IN THE NAME OF
ALLAH
THE ALL-COMPASSIONATE, ALL-MERCIFUL

You Can Be

The Happiest Woman in the World

A Treasure Chest of Reminders

- Title: You Can Be The Happiest Woman in the World
         (A Treasure Chest of Reminders)
- Author: Dr. 'Ā'iḍ al-Qarni
- English Edition 1 (2005)
- Translated from Arabic Edition 2 (2004)
- Translator: Huda Khaṭṭāb
- Layout: IIPH, Riyadh, Saudi Arabia
- Filming & Cover Designing: Samo Press Group

You Can Be
The Happiest Woman in the World
A Treasure Chest of Reminders

Dr. 'Ā'iḍ al-Qarni

Translated by
Huda Khaṭṭāb

INTERNATIONAL ISLAMIC PUBLISHING HOUSE

© **International Islamic Publishing House, 2005**

King Fahd National Library Cataloging-in-Publication Data

Al-Qarni, Aaid
  The happiest woman in the world. / Aaid al-Qarni ; translated
by Huda al-Khattab .- Riyadh, 2005

  ...p ; 22 cm

  ISBN Hard Cover: **9960-850-89-7**
  ISBN Soft Cover : **9960-850-90-0**

  1- Women in Islam   I-Huda al-Khattab (translator)   II-Title

  219.2 dc   1424/7273
                    1424/7274

  ISBN Hard Cover: **9960-850-89-7**   Legal Deposit no. **1424/7273**
  ISBN Soft Cover : **9960-850-90-0**   Legal Deposit no. **1424/7274**

International Islamic Publishing House (IIPH)
P.O.Box 55195 Riyadh 11534, Saudi Arabia
Tel: 966 1 4650818 — 4647213 — Fax: 4633489
E-Mail: iiph@iiph.com.sa — www.iiph.com.sa

*Please take part in this noble work by conveying
your comments to **IIPH** through e-mail,
fax or postal-mail address.*

PUBLISHER'S NOTE

All praise, gratitude and thanks are to Almighty God, the Lord of the worlds; and all prayers and blessings are upon our Prophet Muhammad, his family, Companions and followers.

Based on the grace of Islam, its values and principles, the author of *The Happiest Woman*, Dr. 'Ā'iḍ al-Qarni, with his rich experience and wide knowledge, has compiled in this book a collection of invaluable moral and behavioural recommendations designed for securing the welfare and well-being of Muslim women.

These recommendations are the conclusion of a combination of Qur'anic verses, Prophetic sayings, sincere advice, objective stories, thoughtful ideas and faithful experiments that would guide women to the right path which leads to comfort, content, assurance, love and happiness in this life and in the Hereafter.

The careful assimilation and punctual application of the content of this book, after having steadfast faith in Allah and asking His refuge at times of both ease and hardship, will definitely help every reader not only to achieve the above basic objectives, but also to become among the happiest women on earth.

May Allah, the Exalted, the All-Glorious, reward Dr. al-Qarni for all his good efforts, bless those who contributed to the production of this work and enable readers to benefit from it as intended. *Āmīn* (may Allah accept the same).

Muhammad 'Abdul Muḥsin Al Tuwaijri
International Islamic Publishing House
Riyadh, Saudi Arabia
1425 AH — 2005 CE

DEDICATION

To every Muslim woman who is content with Allah as her Lord, Islam as her religion and Muhammad (Blessings and Peace be upon him) as her Prophet.

To every girl who follows the path of truth, who carries the message of sincerity.

To every teacher who strives by means of her words to convey knowledge and values, and has purified her soul.

To every mother who brings her children up to fear Allah and to follow the Sunnah, and makes virtue dear to them.

To every woman who is burdened with worries and sadness.

Rejoice and receive the glad tidings of a way-out at hand, the care of Allah, a great reward and expiation of sins.

TRANSLATOR'S FOREWORD

The pursuit of happiness — is something that concerns us all, no matter where we live or what our station in life is. In this book, Dr. al-Qarni explores the path to finding happiness. Drawing on Islamic teachings and the wise words of Muslim scholars down throughout the ages, as well as the voices of experts and high achievers from both east and west, he highlights profound truths in brief, easily-grasped segments that anyone can find time to read no matter how busy his life is.

Realistically enough, he makes it quite clear that life in this world will never be perfect (that will only happen in Paradise, of course), but it is within our ability, with the help of Allah, to make the most of what we have in this world and attain a level of contentment and happiness no matter what our lot in life is.

There are important lessons to be learned here: faith, hope, patience and acceptance... and never underestimate the power of a smile.

This is a good book for busy women, regardless of their role in life, whether they are wives, mothers or working women (or all three), containing short, snappy passages that lead to greater truths. Grasp the "sound bites" now, but do not forget to come back to the Islamic legacy to deepen your knowledge of the concepts mentioned here.

May Allah reward the author for his work and for bringing important lessons to busy people.

Huda Khaṭṭāb

INTRODUCTION

Praise be to Allah, the Lord of the Worlds, and blessings and peace be upon the Messenger of Allah and upon his family and Companions and those who follow him.

This book urges the Muslim woman to rejoice in her religion and in the grace that Allah has bestowed upon her. It brings hope and glad tidings to everyone who feels distressed, depressed and burdened with many worries. It invites the Muslim woman to expect a way out and to look forward to ease after hardship. It addresses her rational mind and pure heart, telling her to be patient and seek reward with Allah, do not despair, do not give up, be optimistic, for Allah is with you, Allah is sufficient for you, Allah, the Almighty, will protect you.

My sister, read this book, for it contains clear and unambiguous verses from the Qur'an, true hadiths, sound ideas, inspiring stories and the wisdom of obedience. Read this book and chase away the traces of sadness, the specters of distress, the nightmares of fear and anxiety. Read this book to help you cleanse your mind of the clutter of illusions and devilish whispers, and show you the way to a sense of tranquility, faith, joy and happiness. May Allah give you happiness in this world and in the Hereafter, and bestow His Favour upon you, for He is the Most Generous, Most Kind.

I have presented this book as a treasure chest filled with beautiful ideas with which you may adorn your life. It contains pearls of beauty and truth that surpass the brilliant lure of gold and silver.

If you have this book in your hands, you should not care about any worldly adornments, empty decorations, false appearances or transient fashions. Adorn yourself with these treasures and wear them on all special occasions in life, at all times of joy and celebration, so that you will be — if Allah wills — the happiest woman in the world.

The way to happiness is to be found in clarity of knowledge and soundness of education. This cannot be achieved by reading romantic fiction that takes the reader away from reality and is filled with rosy dreams and dizzying illusions, but which leads to frustration and depression. Indeed, the matter is even more serious than that, such as the stories of Agatha Christie, which teach about deceit, crime and robbery. I have read the series entitled *The Best of World Fiction*, a selection of exciting, Nobel Prize-winning stories, and I found that these stories contained many serious mistakes and a great deal of foolishness. Undoubtedly, some of the best of world fiction includes some stories that are good from a purely artistic point of view and with regard to the skill of storytelling, such as *The Old Man and the Sea* by Earnest Hemingway, and other such stories that avoid immoral content, decadence and other signs of literary decline.

Every wise woman should read the books of our sound (Arabic and Islamic) literary heritage, such as the books of aṭ-Ṭanṭāwī, al-Kīlāni, al-Manfalūṭi, ar-Rāfiʻi and so on, those of a pure and clear conscience who carry a clear message. I have only mentioned this because I am keen for my book to be free of any foreign influence, deviation or trivia. How many people have fallen victims to articles or stories that they have read. And Allah, the All-Glorious, is the One Whose protection we seek.

Whatever the case, there is nothing better than the stories told by Allah in His Book, and by His Messenger in the Sunnah, and the glorious history of the righteous, the caliphs, scholars and pious people. So be of good cheer and rejoice in the blessing of Allah, for you are blessed in your religion and guidance, your *'aqīdah* (belief) and heritage.

Dr. 'Ā'iḍ al-Qarni

Chapter 1

WELCOME!

Welcome, O' devout, Allah-fearing woman who prays and fasts.

Welcome, O' wise, dignified woman who observes *ḥijāb*.

Welcome, O' aware, well-read and educated woman.

Welcome, O' charitable, sincere, trustworthy and loyal woman.

Welcome, O' patient woman who seeks reward from Allah, repenting and turning to Him.

Welcome, O' woman who remembers Allah and gives thanks to Him, and calls upon Him.

Welcome, O' woman who follows the footsteps of Āsiyah, Maryam and Khadījah.

Welcome, O' mother of heroes and producer of men.

Welcome, O' cherisher and guardian of values.

Welcome, O' woman who heeds the sacred limits of Allah and keeps away from forbidden things.

YES!

Yes to your beautiful smile that sends a message of warmth and friendliness to others.

Yes to your kind words that establish friendship as permitted in Islam and dispel rancour.

Yes to acceptable charity that brings happiness to the poor and feeds the hungry.

Yes to sitting with the Qur'an, reciting it, pondering its meanings and acting upon them, and repenting and seeking forgiveness.

Yes to remembering Allah a great deal and praying for forgiveness, persisting in *du'ā'* and offering sincere repentance.

Yes to raising your children in Islam, teaching them the Sunnah and guiding them to that which will benefit them.

Yes to modesty and *ḥijāb* as enjoined by Allah, which is the means of self-protection.

Yes to the friendship of good women who fear Allah, love Islam and respect high values.

Yes to honouring one's parents, upholding the ties of kinship, honouring one's neighbours and caring for orphans.

Yes to reading useful, interesting and beneficial books.

NO!

No to wasting time in trivial pursuits, and love of revenge and futile arguments.

No to giving priority to money and accumulation of wealth over one's health, happiness, sleep and peace of mind.

No to seeking out other people's faults and backbiting about them, whilst forgetting one's own faults.

No to indulging in physical pleasure and giving in to every whim and desire.

No to wasting time with shallow people and spending hours in idle pursuits.

No to neglecting physical hygiene and cleanliness in the house, and being disorganized at home.

No to *ḥarām* drinks, cigarettes, narghile ("hookah pipes"), and all foul things.

No to thinking of past calamities and dwelling on past mistakes.

No to forgetting the Hereafter and neglecting to strive for it, and to being careless of what will happen in the Hereafter.

No to wasting money on *ḥarām* things, being extravagant with regard to permissible things, and falling short in acts of worship.

TEN THOUGHTS TO PONDER

1. Remember that your Lord forgives those who ask Him for forgiveness, and He accepts the repentance of those who repent, and He accepts those who come back to Him.

2. Show mercy to the weak and you will be happy; give to the needy and you will be well; do not bear grudges and you will be healthy.

3. Be optimistic, for Allah is with you, and the angels are praying for forgiveness for you, and Paradise awaits you.

4. Wipe away your tears, think well of your Lord, and chase away your worries by remembering the blessings that Allah has bestowed upon you.

5. Do not think that this world is ever perfect for anyone. There is no one on the face of the earth who gets all that he wants or is free from all kinds of distress.

6. Be like a tall tree with high aims; if a stone is thrown at it, it simply lets its fruits drop.

7. Have you ever heard that grief brings back what has been lost, or that worry corrects mistakes? So why grieve and worry then?

8. Do not expect trials and calamities, rather expect peace, safety and good health, if Allah wills.

9. Extinguish the flames of hatred from your heart by forgiving everyone who has ever hurt you.

10. *Ghusl, wuḍū', siwāk* and being organized are effective medicines for all kinds of distress and worry.

THINK ABOUT IT...

1. Be like the bee, which lands on fragrant flowers and fresh branches.

2. You do not have time to seek out people's defects and mistakes.

3. If Allah is with you, then whom do you have to fear? If Allah is against you, then what hope do you have?

4. The fire of envy consumes the body, and excessive jealousy is like a raging fire.

5. If you do not prepare today, then you will not be able to do anything tomorrow.

6. Withdraw peacefully from places where idle arguments are going on.

7. Let your morals and attitudes be even more beautiful than a garden.

8. Do acts of kindness and you will be the happiest of people.

9. Leave people to their Creator, leave the envier to death, and forget about your enemy.

10. The pleasure of *ḥarām* actions is followed by regret, loss and punishment.

Chapter 2

"There is no power and no strength except with Allah."

1
A woman who challenged tyranny

The past is gone and the hoped-for future is still unknown. All you have is the present.

Look at the texts of Islam, the Qur'an and Sunnah. Allah, the Exalted, the Almighty, praises righteous and believing women. He says:

﴿وَضَرَبَ ٱللَّهُ مَثَلًا لِّلَّذِينَ ءَامَنُواْ ٱمْرَأَتَ فِرْعَوْنَ إِذْ قَالَتْ رَبِّ ٱبْنِ لِي عِندَكَ بَيْتًا فِي ٱلْجَنَّةِ وَنَجِّنِي مِن فِرْعَوْنَ وَعَمَلِهِۦ وَنَجِّنِي مِنَ ٱلْقَوْمِ ٱلظَّٰلِمِينَ ﴾ ⟨١١⟩

(سورة التحْريم: ١١)

❨And Allah has set forth an example for those who believe: the wife of Fir'awn [Pharaoh], when she said: 'My Lord! Build for me a home with You in Paradise, and save me from Fir'awn [Pharaoh] and his work, and save me from the people who are *Zālimūn* [polytheists, wrongdoers and disbelievers in Allah].'❩   *(Qur'an 66: 11)*

Think about how Allah made this woman — Āsiyah, may Allah be pleased with her — a living example for believing men and women, a clear symbol for everyone who wants to be guided and follow the ways of Allah in life. How wise this woman was, when she sought a home with the Lord and put that above her worldly interests. She freed herself from the control of the *kāfir* (disbeliever) tyrant Pharaoh and refused to live in his palace with his servants and courtiers, and with all its luxuries. She sought a better home that was more lasting and more beautiful, with the Lord of the Worlds, amidst gardens and rivers, in a seat of truth (i.e. Paradise), near the Omnipotent King (Allah, the One, the All-Blessed, the Most High, the Owner of Majesty and Honour) *(Qur'an 54: 55)*. She was a great woman whose ambition and sincerity led her to speak the word of truth and faith against her tyrant husband. She was tortured for the sake of Allah but she ultimately earned a home with the Lord of the Worlds, and Allah the Exalted, made her an example for every believing man and woman until the Hour comes, and He praised her in His Book, recording her name and commending her deeds, and condemning her husband who deviated from the right path on earth.

"Be optimistic, even if you are in the eye of the storm."

❨Verily with every difficulty there is relief.❩
(Qur'an 94: 6)

2
You have a huge wealth of blessings

My sister, verily with every difficulty there is ease *(Qur'an 94: 6)*; after night comes the day. The clouds of worry will be blown away, the darkness of distress will be dispelled, and calamities will come to an end, by Allah's leave. Remember that you will be rewarded, and if you are a mother, your children will be a great support and help for Islam, if you bring them up properly. They will make *du'ā'* for you when they prostrate and at the end of the night, just before dawn. It is a great blessing if you are a compassionate and kind mother. It is sufficient honour and pride for you to remember that the mother of Muhammad (Blessings and Peace be upon him) gave mankind a great leader, the noble Messenger.

You have the potential to be a *dā'iyah* (caller to Islam) calling other women to the path of Allah with kind words, good exhortation and wisdom, arguing in a manner that is better, debating and guiding others by means of your good behaviour and setting an example. A woman may achieve, by means of her conduct and righteous deeds, things that cannot be achieved by means of *khuṭbahs* (religious sermons), lectures and lessons. How often has a woman gone to live in a neighbourhood, and people started to talk about her religious commitment, modesty, *ḥijāb* (Islamic dress) and good attitude, her kindness to her neighbours and her obedience to her husband, so she became a good example to others, that was spoken of by all.

> "Soon the flowers will bloom, grief will depart and happiness will prevail."

❲... After hardship, Allah will soon grant relief.❳

(Qur'an 65: 7)

3
It is sufficient honour for you that you are a Muslim

Everything that happens to you for the sake of Allah is an expiation for you, if Allah, the Exalted, wills. Hear the glad tidings narrated in the hadith:

"If a woman obeys her Lord, offers her five daily prayers and preserves her honour, she will enter the Paradise of her Lord."

These are easy matters for the one for whom Allah makes them easy. So, by doing these great deeds you will meet a merciful Lord who will give you happiness in this world and in the Hereafter. Follow His laws no matter where that leads you, and adhere to the Book of Allah (the Qur'an) and the Sunnah of His Messenger Muhammad (Blessings and Peace be upon him), for you are a Muslim woman, and this is a great honour and source of pride. Other women were born in the lands of *kufr* (disbelief), Christians, Jews, Communists or something other than the religion of Islam, but Allah chose you to be a Muslim woman, and He made you one of the followers of Muhammad (Blessings and Peace be upon him), following in the footsteps of 'Ā'ishah, Khadījah and Fāṭimah — may Allah be pleased with them all. Congratulations, for you offer the five daily prayers, you fast Ramaḍān, you go on pilgrimage to the House, you observe Islamic *ḥijāb*. Congratulations, for you are pleased with Allah as your Lord, Islam as your religion, and Muhammad (Blessings and

Peace be upon him) as your Prophet.

"Your gold is your religion, your adornment is your moral attitude, and your wealth is your good manners."

❨... Allah is sufficient for us and He is
the best disposer of affairs.❩ *(Qur'an 3: 173)*

4
The believing woman and the disbelieving woman are not equal

You can be happy if you examine just one issue — the situation of the Muslim woman in the Muslim lands and the situation of the disbelieving woman in the lands of disbelief. The Muslim woman in the Muslim land is a believing woman who gives charity, fasts, prays *qiyām al-Layl* (night prayers), observes *ḥijāb*, obeys her husband, fears her Lord, is kind to her neighbours and is compassionate towards her children. So she is to be congratulated for her great reward, tranquility and contentment. The disbelieving woman in the lands of disbelief is a woman who makes a wanton display of herself; she is ignorant and foolish, a mere fashion model, a cheap and worthless product on offer in all places. She has no value, honour or religion. Compare the two situations, and you will see that you are the happiest, the most well off. Praise be to Allah, the Almighty.

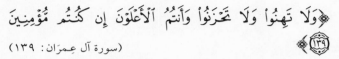

(سورة آل عِمرَان: ١٣٩)

❨So do not become weak [against your enemy], nor be sad, and you will be superior [in victory] if you are indeed [true] believers.❩ *(Qur'an 3: 139)*

"All people will live, the one who lives

in a palace and the one who lives in a hovel. But who is the one who is happy?"

"Allah is my Lord and I do not associate anything with Him."

5
Laziness is kin to failure

I urge you to keep busy, not to give in to laziness and idleness. Rather, you should take care of your house and home library, and do your duties and your work, or pray, or read Qur'an or useful books, or listen to useful tapes, or sit with your neighbours and friends and talk to them about things that will bring them closer to Allah. Then you will find happiness and joy, by Allah's Leave. And beware of giving in to idleness, for this will lead to worries, anxiety, devilish whispers and doubts that nothing can relieve except hard work.

You should take care of your appearance, wear perfume at home, keep your house tidy, and meet your husband, children, siblings, relatives and friends looking cheerful, with a ready smile and an attitude of contentment.

Beware of sin for it leads to grief, especially the sins that are very common among women, such as forbidden glances, wanton adornment, being alone with a non-*mahram* man, cursing, slandering, backbiting, denying one's husband's rights and not acknowledging his acts of kindness. These sins are very common among women, except for those on whom Allah has mercy, so beware of incurring the wrath of Allah and fear Him, for fear of Allah is what brings happiness and a clear conscience.

"When distress strikes and calamities come one after another, then say: *Lā ilāha illallah."*

❨... Patience is most fitting...❩

(Qur'an 12: 18)

6

You are better off than millions of women

Think of the world as a whole, of the hospitals filled with patients who have been stricken with disease and calamity for many years; and the prisons in which thousands of people are held behind bars, their lives and pleasures ruined; and the asylums and hospitals which accommodate people who have lost their minds and have become insane. Are there not poor people living in tattered tents and hovels, who cannot find a bite to eat? Are there not women who have been stricken with calamities that took away all their children in a single accident? Or women who have lost their sight or hearing, or whose arms or legs have been amputated, or who have lost their minds, or who have been stricken with chronic diseases such as cancer and the like? But you are sound in body and in good health, living a life of tranquility, security and contentment. So give thanks to Allah, the Exalted, All-Merciful, for His blessings and do not waste your time with things that are not pleasing to Him, sitting for hours in front of satellite TV with its cheap, nasty and foolish content that makes the heart sick and causes depression, and makes the body lethargic. Rather, choose that which is useful and beneficial, such as lectures and conferences, or programmes about medicine, or news that concerns Muslims, men and women, and so on. Avoid this garbage that is shown and this promiscuity that they are trying to spread, for it destroys modesty and religious commitment.

"Leave the wrongdoer to the court of
the Hereafter when there will be no
judge but Allah."

"From one minute to the next there could come a way out."

7
Build yourself a palace in Paradise

Look how many generations have passed away. Did they take their wealth with them? Did they take their palaces and their high status? Were they buried with their gold and silver? Did they take their cars and planes with them to the Hereafter? No! They were stripped even of their clothing, and placed in their graves in their shrouds, then each of them was asked: Who is your Lord, who is your Prophet, what is your religion? So prepare yourself for that day; do not grieve or despair about any worldly comforts, for they are cheap and transient. Nothing will abide except righteous deeds. Allah, the Exalted, says:

﴿مَنْ عَمِلَ صَالِحًا مِّن ذَكَرٍ أَوْ أُنثَىٰ وَهُوَ مُؤْمِنٌ فَلَنُحْيِيَنَّهُ حَيَوٰةً طَيِّبَةً وَلَنَجْزِيَنَّهُمْ أَجْرَهُم بِأَحْسَنِ مَا كَانُوا۟ يَعْمَلُونَ ﴿٩٧﴾

(سورة النحل : ٩٧)

﴿Whoever works righteousness — whether male or female — while he [or she] is a true believer [of Islamic Monotheism] verily, to him We will give a good life [in this world with respect, contentment and lawful provision], and We shall pay them certainly a reward in proportion to the best of what they used to do [i.e. Paradise in the Hereafter].﴾ *(Qur'an 16: 97)*

"Sickness is a message in which there is a glad tiding, and good health is a garment that has a price."

❨... There is no god but You, glory to You,
verily I was among the wrongdoers.❩

(Qur'an 21: 87)

8
Do not destroy your heart
with your own hands

Avoid everything that wastes time, such as looking at immoral magazines, indecent pictures, bad ideas, heretical books or immoral stories. You should seek out that which is beneficial and useful, such as Islamic magazines, beneficial books and articles that will benefit a person both in this world and in the Hereafter. Some books and magazines instill doubts in the heart and lead one astray. This is the effect of the decadent culture that has been imported to us from the world of disbelief and has spread throughout the Muslim world.

Remember that with Allah are the keys of the unseen, and He, the Almighty, All-Merciful, is the One Who brings relief from worry and distress. So turn to Him and call upon Him, and always repeat this *du'ā'*:

"*Allahumma inni a'ūdhu bika min al-hammi wal-ḥazan wa a'ūdhu bika min al-'ajzi wal-kasal wa a'ūdhu bika min al-bukhli wal-jubn wa a'ūdhu bika min ghalbat ad-dayn wa qahr ar-rijāl* (O' Allah, I seek refuge with You from distress and grief, and I seek refuge with You from incapacity and laziness, and I seek refuge with You from miserliness and cowardice, and I seek refuge in You from the burden of debt and from being over-powered by men)."

If you repeat this often and ponder its meaning, Allah, the Almighty, All-Gracious, will grant you a way out of your distress and worry, by His Leave.

> "Plant a *tasbīḥ* (saying *Subḥān Allah*) in a second, an idea in a minute, and a deed in an hour."

❨Is not He [better than your gods] Who
responds to the distressed one...❩ *(Qur'an 27: 62)*

9
You are dealing with a Lord Who is Most Kind and Most Generous

Be of good cheer, for Allah, the Exalted, has promised you
a great reward, as He says:

$$﴿فَٱسْتَجَابَ لَهُمْ رَبُّهُمْ أَنِّي لَا أُضِيعُ عَمَلَ عَامِلٍ مِّنكُم مِّن ذَكَرٍ أَوْ أُنثَىٰ ... ﴿١٩٥﴾ ﴾$$

(سورة آل عِمرَان: ١٩٥)

❨So their Lord accepted of them [their supplication
and answered them], 'Never will I allow to be lost the
work of any of you, be he male or female.'❩

(Qur'an 3: 195)

Allah has given the same promises to men as to women, and
He praises women as He praises men:

$$﴿إِنَّ ٱلْمُسْلِمِينَ وَٱلْمُسْلِمَٰتِ وَٱلْمُؤْمِنِينَ وَٱلْمُؤْمِنَٰتِ وَٱلْقَٰنِتِينَ وَٱلْقَٰنِتَٰتِ وَٱلصَّٰدِقِينَ وَٱلصَّٰدِقَٰتِ وَٱلصَّٰبِرِينَ وَٱلصَّٰبِرَٰتِ وَٱلْخَٰشِعِينَ وَٱلْخَٰشِعَٰتِ وَٱلْمُتَصَدِّقِينَ وَٱلْمُتَصَدِّقَٰتِ وَٱلصَّٰئِمِينَ وَٱلصَّٰئِمَٰتِ وَٱلْحَٰفِظِينَ فُرُوجَهُمْ وَٱلْحَٰفِظَٰتِ وَٱلذَّٰكِرِينَ ٱللَّهَ كَثِيرًا وَٱلذَّٰكِرَٰتِ أَعَدَّ ٱللَّهُ لَهُم مَّغْفِرَةً وَأَجْرًا عَظِيمًا﴾$$

(سورة الأحزَاب: ٣٥)

❨Verily, the Muslims [those who submit to Allah in

Islam] men and women, the believers, men and women [who believe in Islamic Monotheism], the men and the women who are obedient [to Allah], the men and women who are truthful [in their speech and deeds], the men and the women who are patient [in performing all the duties which Allah has ordered and in abstaining from all that Allah has forbidden], the men and the women who are humble [before their Lord, Allah], the men and the women who give *Ṣadaqāt* [i.e. *Zakāh* and alms], the men and the women who observe *Ṣawm* [the obligatory fasting during the month of Ramaḍān, and the optional *Nawafil* (voluntary) fasting], the men and the women who guard their chastity [from illegal sexual acts] and the men and the women who remember Allah much with their hearts and tongues. Allah has prepared for them forgiveness and a great reward [i.e. Paradise].

(Qur'an 33: 35)

This indicates that women are the twin halves and companions of men, and that your reward is stored with Allah. You can do good deeds at home and in society, that will help you attain the pleasure of Allah. So, set the best of examples and be a beacon for the children of the *Ummah*.

Take your cue from the life of Āsiyah, the wife of Pharaoh, may Allah be pleased with her, and Maryam (may peace be upon her), Khadījah, 'Ā'ishah, Asmā' and Fāṭimah (may Allah be pleased with them). These were chosen women, devout believers who fasted and prayed at night. May Allah be pleased with them and grant them great reward. Follow their footsteps and you will find tranquility and dignity.

"Wipe away the tears of the orphan in

order to attain the pleasure of the
Most Merciful and a house in
Paradise."

"Is not morning close at hand?"

10
You will be the winner in all situations

You have to seek reward with Allah. If some worry, distress or grief befalls you, remember that it is an expiation for sin. If you lose one of your children, remember that he will intercede for you before Allah. If some disability or sickness befalls you, remember that it brings its own reward from Allah, which is preserved with Him. Hunger, sickness and poverty all bring their own rewards from Allah. Nothing is ever lost with Him. He keeps it as a trust with Him until He gives it to its owner in the Hereafter.

"Prayer is guaranteed to bring tranquility and chase away worry."

Chapter 3

⟪... Take what comes to you and give thanks.⟫

(Qur'an 7: 144)

1
Count the blessings that Allah has bestowed upon you

When morning comes, remember that the sun is shining upon thousands of miserable women, but you are blessed; it is shining on hundreds of hungry women, but you have plenty to eat; it shines on thousands of women who are imprisoned, but you are free; it shines on thousands of women who have been stricken with calamity and lost their children, but you are happy and healthy. How many tears flow down women's cheeks, how many mothers' hearts are filled with pain, how many screams come from girls' throats — but you are smiling and happy. So praise Allah, the Exalted, for His kindness, protection and generosity.

Sit and think, and be honest with yourself; look at the numbers and statistics. How many things do you own, how much wealth do you possess, how many blessings do you enjoy, how many things do you have that bring you delight? Beauty, wealth, children, shade, a home, a country, light, air, water, nourishment, medicine? Rejoice and be of good cheer.

"Buy with charity the *du'ā'* and love of the poor and needy."

"Be content with that which Allah has decreed for you,
and you will be the richest of people."

2
A little that makes you happy is better than a lot that makes you miserable

The part of your life that really counts is that in which you are happy and contented. As for greed and panic, they do not count at all. They are bad for your health and rob you of your beauty. Remain content with Allah and with what is decreed for you; believe in *al-qadar* (the divine decree) and be optimistic about the future. Be like a butterfly, which is light-hearted and beautiful, not attached to mere things; it flies from flower to flower, from hill to hill, from garden to garden. Or be like a bee, which eats good things and produces good things; when it lands on a branch or flower, it does not break it; it takes the nectar and does not sting, and produces honey and does not sting, and buzzes with love and glad tidings, reflecting a sense of contentment, as if it is a heavenly creature that has come down to earth.

"Allah loves those who repent and turn to Him."

"Praise be to Allah Who has taken away my grief."

3
Look at the clouds and not at the ground

Be ambitious, keep climbing and always have hope. Beware of falling, and remember that life is minutes and seconds. Be like the ant in hard work, patience and perseverance. Always keep trying, and keep repenting. If you go back to sin, then repent again. Memorize Qur'an, and if you forget it, go back and memorize it again and again. The main thing is that you should never feel defeated or frustrated, because rationally speaking there is no such thing as the last word or the bitter end, rather there is always trial and error, and learning from your mistakes. Life is like a body that may undergo cosmetic surgery; it is like a building that can be renovated and rebuilt from scratch, with new decor and paint. Do away with all thoughts of failure, and stop thinking of calamities and problems, for Allah, the Almighty, says:

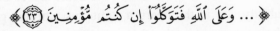

(سورة المَائدة: ٢٣)

❴... and put your trust in Allah if you are indeed believers.❵　　　　*(Qur'an 5: 23)*

"Giving up sin is jihād (fighting in Allah's Cause), but persisting in it is stubbornness."

❴And give glad tidings to those who believe...❵

(Qur'an 2: 25)

4
Living in a hut with faith is better than living in a palace with disbelief

A Muslim woman living in a hut, worshipping her Lord, offering her five daily prayers and fasting Ramaḍān, is happier than a woman who lives in a lofty palace with servants and all means of luxuries. A believing woman living in a tent and eating barley bread and drinking water from an earthenware jar, who has her *Muṣḥaf* and *masbaḥah* (Muslim rosary) with her, is better off than a woman who lives in an ivory tower in rooms furnished with velvet, but who does not know her Lord or follow her Prophet. You should understand the true meaning of happiness: it is not the narrow and distorted meaning that many people imagine. Do you think that happiness is to be found in dollars and *dinars*, furnishings and clothing, food and drink, means of transportation? Not at all. Happiness is contentment in the heart, peace of mind, a sense of stability, joy in the heart, a righteous attitude, good behaviour and being content with what is sufficient.

"How can he feel relaxed or content,
who harms a Muslim or a slave?"

"Put your trust in the Ever-Living
Who will never die."

5
Organize your time so that you can do all you have to do

Try reading a good book or listening to a useful tape. Listen to a beautiful recitation of the Book of Allah — perhaps a single verse will penetrate deeply in your heart and stir your conscience, bringing guidance and light, and dispelling doubts and despair. Read the books of Sunnah and the words of the Prophet (Blessings and Peace be upon him) in *Riyāḍ aṣ-Ṣāliḥīn*. You will find the correct remedy and beneficial knowledge which will protect you from slipping or making mistakes, and will solve all your problems. Your medicine is in the Revelation, the Qur'an and Sunnah, your comfort is in faith, your delight in prayer, your peace of mind in contentment, the beauty of your face in smiling, the protection of your honour in *ḥijāb*, and your tranquility in *dhikr* (remembrance of Allah, the All-Merciful).

"Beware of the *du'ā'* of the one who has been wronged and the tears of the one who has been deprived."

❴In order that you may not be sad over matters
that you fail to get, nor rejoice because of that
which has been given to you...❵

(Qur'an 57: 23)

6
Our happiness is not like theirs

Who told you that distracting music, immoral songs, cheap soap operas, reprehensible plays, offensive magazines and dubious movies bring happiness and joy? Whoever told you that, is lying! These are things that lead to misery, depression and distress, as acknowledged by those who have worked in those fields and then repented. So flee from this miserable life of idlers who deviate from the straight path of Allah, and come to recitation of the Qur'an with humility, useful books, moving lessons, stirring *khutbahs* (sermons), true friendship, sincere repentance. Come to spiritual gatherings and remembrance of Allah; may He accept your repentance and fill your heart with tranquility and peace.

"In the sound heart there is no room for *shirk* (polytheism), deceit, rancour or envy."

❨O' my Lord! Expand for me my breast [grant me self-confidence, contentment, and boldness].❩

(Qur'an 20: 25)

7
Climb aboard the ship of salvation

I have read the stories of dozens of actors, singers and others who were involved in idle pursuits, both living and dead, and I said: What a shame! Where are the Muslim men and women, the believing men and women, the sincere men and women, the men and women who fast, the men and women who worship Allāh, the Exalted, the men and women who are humble and devout? Can this short life be wasted on idle matters and trivial pursuits? Do you have another life besides this one? Do you have a promise from Allah that you will never die? No, by Allah. These are just false illusions and wishful thinking. Take stock of yourself, then, and draw up a new plan; strive hard to catch up and climb aboard the ship of salvation.

"The wise woman turns a desert into a beautiful garden."

"Ease comes after hardship."

8
The key to happiness is prostration

The first step towards happiness each day is *Fajr* (Dawn) prayer, so start your day with it, then you will be under the protection and care of Allah, the Almighty; He will protect you from all evils and guide you to all that is good. Allah does not bless a day that does not start with *Fajr*. It is the first step towards acceptance and success. So, glad tidings to all those who pray *Fajr*, and misery and loss to those who neglect this prayer.

"Futile arguments and trivial discussions take away the sense of peace and tranquility."

❰Have We not expanded for you your breast?❱

(Qur'an 94: 1)

9
Old women make heroes

Be like the old woman before al-Ḥajjāj, who put her trust in her Lord when al-Ḥajjāj put her son in prison and swore to her by Allah that he was going to kill him. She said, with confidence and courage, "If you do not kill him, he will die anyway!"

Be like the old Persian woman who put her trust in Allah the day she had to be away from her chicken coop. She looked up towards the heavens and said: "O' Allah, protect my chicken coop for You are the Best of protectors!"

Be steadfast like Asmā' bint Abi Bakr, who saw her son 'Abdallāh ibn az-Zubayr crucified, and said her famous words: "Is it not time for this knight to dismount (i.e., come down off the crucifixion post)?"

Be like al-Khansā' who offered four martyrs for the sake of Allah, and when they were killed she said: "Praise be to Allah Who has honoured me by causing them to be slain as martyrs for His sake." Look at these woman and their glorious history.

"Take from the breeze its tenderness, from the musk its fragrance and from the mountain its steadfastness."

❨So do not become weak [against your enemy], nor be sad, and you will be superior [in victory]...❩ *(Qur'an 3: 139)*

10
To be the most beautiful woman in the world

With your beauty, you are better than the sun; with your morals you are more sublime than musk; with your modesty you are nobler than the full moon; with your compassion you are more beneficial than rain. So, preserve your beauty with faith, your tranquility with contentment, your chastity with *ḥijāb*. Remember that your adornment is not gold, silver or diamonds, rather, it is two *rak'ahs* at *Fajr*, going thirsty when you fast for Allah, concealed charity which no one knows except Him, hot tears that wash away sin, a lengthy prostration born of utter submission to Allah, shyness before Allah when the inclination to do evil overwhelms you. Clothe yourself with the garments of *taqwā* (piety) for you are the most beautiful woman in the world, even if your clothes are shabby. Clothe yourself with the cloak of modesty, for you are the most beautiful woman in the world even if you are barefoot. Beware of the life of bewitching immoral disbelieving women, for they are the fuel of the fire of Hell.

﴿لَا يَصْلَىٰهَآ إِلَّا ٱلْأَشْقَى ۝﴾   (سورة الليل: ١٥)

❨None shall enter it save the most wretched.❩*(Qur'an 92: 15)*

> "Wherever you go and find darkness in your life; what you have to do is to light the lamp within yourself."

Chapter 4

"When you wake up in the morning,
do not expect to live until evening."

1
You (are) notable and honourable

O' sincere Muslim, O' believing woman who constantly turns to Allah, the Exalted, be like the palm tree and rise above evil and harm; if a stone is thrown at the palm tree, it lets its fruit drop (and does not retaliate). It remains green summer and winter, and gives many benefits. Do not lower yourself to the level of trivial matters, and rise above all that may damage your modesty and honour. Your words should be *dhikr*, your glance should teach you something, your silence should be contemplation. Then you will find happiness and peace of mind; you will be well accepted and people will shower praise on you and make *du'ā'* for you, and Allah will take away the clouds of rancour, the specters of fear and the clutter of depression. Go to sleep secure with the knowledge that the believers are praying for you, and wake up to their praise of you. Then you will realize that happiness does not mean having a lot of money in the bank, rather, it is to be found in obeying Allah; it is not to be found in wearing new clothes or serving people, rather, it is to be found in obeying Allah.

"Do not give up on yourself, because change is usually slow; you will encounter obstacles that will discourage you, but do not let these obstacles defeat you."

❬... Invoke Me, I will respond to your [invocation]...❭

(Qur'an 40: 60)

2
Accept the blessing and make the most of it

Make the most of the blessings of Allah, give thanks to Him and obey Him. Enjoy the water that you drink and use for *wuḍū'*. Enjoy the warmth and light of the sun, and the light and beauty of the moon. Pick fruit from the trees, drink your fill from the rivers, look at the ocean, walk through the fields, and give thanks to Allah, the Almighty, Oft-Forgiving, the Sovereign and Subduer. Make use of these blessings that Allah has bestowed upon you, and beware of denying these blessings.

﴿ ۞ ... يَعْرِفُونَ نِعْمَتَ ٱللَّهِ ثُمَّ يُنكِرُونَهَا ﴾

(سورة النَّحل: ٨٣)

❬They recognize the Grace of Allah, yet they deny it...❭

(Qur'an 16: 83)

Before you look at the thorn of the rose, look at its beauty. Before you complain about the heat of the sun, enjoy its light. Before you complain about the blackness of the night, think of its peace and quiet. Why look at things in such a pessimistic and negative manner? Why deny and change blessings?

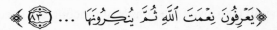

﴿ ۞ أَلَمْ تَرَ إِلَى ٱلَّذِينَ بَدَّلُواْ نِعْمَتَ ٱللَّهِ كُفْرًا ... ﴾

(سورة إبراهيم: ٢٨)

❨Have you not seen those who have changed the Blessings of Allah into disbelief...?❩ *(Qur'an 14: 28)*

Take these blessings and accept them graciously, and praise Allah, the Almighty, All-Glorious, for them.

> "Changing from bad to good is a long-term adventure, but it is wonderful."

❨... Do not despair of the mercy of Allah...❩ *(Qur'an 39: 53)*

3

A great deal of provision comes with seeking forgiveness

A woman said: "My husband died when I was in my thirties, and I had five children, boys and girls, from him. My world turned dark around me, and I wept until I feared I would lose my sight. I complained about my bad luck and fell into despair and depression. My children were small, and our income was not sufficient. I was spending carefully from the little money that our father had left to us. One day in my room, I turned on the radio, and tuned into the Holy Qur'an radio station. I heard a Shaykh saying: "The Messenger of Allah (Blessings and Peace be upon him) said: *'Whoever prays to Allah a great deal for forgiveness, Allah will grant him relief from every distress and a way out from every hardship.'*" So after that I began to pray a great deal for forgiveness, and I told my children to do likewise. Only six months later, the developers came, bought some old property of ours, and paid us millions for it. My son became the first student in his region to memorize the entire Qur'an, and he became a focus of people's care. Our house was filled with blessings and we attained the best standard of living. Allah has kept all my sons and daughters safe and sound, and has taken away my worry, grief and depression. I have become the happiest of women."

"If you give in to despair, you will learn nothing and you will never find happiness."

❨... Certainly no one despairs of Allah's Mercy,

except the people who disbelieve.❩

(Qur'an 12: 87)

4
Du'ā' (invocation) relieves distress

I have a righteous, devout friend whose wife was stricken with cancer. They had three children. He fell into despair and his world turned dark. One of the scholars advised him to pray *qiyām al-layl* and make *du'ā'* in the last part of the night, before dawn, as well as praying for forgiveness and reciting Qur'an over Zamzam water for his wife. He continued to do these things, and his wife started to wash with that Zamzam water over which the Qur'an had been recited. He used to sit with her from *Fajr* until sunrise, then from *Maghrib* (sunset) until *'Ishā'* (evening), asking Allah for forgiveness and supplicating to Him. Then Allah took away her sickness and healed her, and made her hair and skin more beautiful than they had been before, and she became attached to praying for forgiveness and praying *qiyām al-layl*. Glory be to the Healer, the Giver of good health; there is no god but Him and no Lord besides Him.

O' my sister! If you fall sick then turn to Allah, the Almighty, and pray to Him a great deal for forgiveness and call upon Him and repent to Him. Be for good cheer, for Allah answers prayers, relieves distress and takes away bad things.

❨أَمَّن يُجِيبُ ٱلْمُضْطَرَّ إِذَا دَعَاهُ ... ❩ (سورة النَّمل: ٦٢)

❨Is not He [better than your gods] Who responds to

the distressed one, when he calls on Him...?﴿

(Qur'an 27: 62)

"Check your past and your present,
for life is a sequence of experiences
from which one should emerge
victorious."

❨... And He is Ever Most Merciful to the believers.❩

(Qur'an 33: 43)

5
Beware of despair and frustration

A young man was jailed and his mother had no one else but him. She could not sleep and distress took hold of her completely. She wept until she could weep no more, then Allah guided her to say, "*Lā ḥawla wa lā quwwata illā Billāh* (there is no power and no strength except with Allah)." She repeated these great words, which are one of the treasures of Paradise, and only a few days after she had despaired of her son ever coming out of jail, he was knocking at the door and she was filled with joy. Such is the reward of the one who puts his trust in Allah, calls upon Him constantly and delegates all his affairs to Him. So you should recite this *dhikr*, "*Lā ḥawla wa lā quwwata illā Billāh* (there is no power and no strength except with Allah)," for these great words, are the secret of happiness and success. Recite them a great deal, chase away the specters of grief and distress with them, and receive the glad tidings that Allah will soon grant you happiness and a way out. Beware of losing hope or becoming frustrated, for there is no hardship but it is followed by ease. This is how it has always been and there is no need to discuss it. Think positively of Allah, the Exalted, and put your trust in Him; seek that which is with Him, and wait for a way out.

"Do not make your problems the subject of conversation with others, for by doing so you create a barrier between yourself and happiness."

❨... Verily, your Lord is of vast forgiveness...❩

(Qur'an 53: 32)

6
Your house is a kingdom of glory and love

My dear sister! Stay in your home except for serious and necessary matters, for your home is the secret of your happiness.

❨And stay in your houses...❩   *(Qur'an 33: 33)*

In your home, you will find a sense of happiness and you will protect your honour, dignity and modesty, for the insignificant woman is the one who goes to the market frequently for no reason, and whose main concern is to watch trends and follow fashion, going into stores and asking about every new thing. She has no concern for religion or *da'wah* and no ambition to pursue knowledge and become educated. Rather, she is extravagant and her main concern is food and dress. So, beware of forsaking your home, because it is the place of happiness, safety and tranquility, the sanctuary that gives a sense of protection. Make your home a focus of love, generosity and goodness.

> "Do not complain about your problems except to those who can help you with their advice and kind words."

*"How wonderful is the situation of the believer,
for his affairs are all good." (Hadith)*

7
You do not have time for idle talk

Avoid arguments and getting involved in futile discussions about things that may never happen, because that causes anxiety and annoyance. Do not always try to convince people about matters that are open to different points of view, rather, simply state your view quietly without getting angry or trying to pressurize others. Avoid refuting or criticizing others too much, for that will make you feel uneasy and give others the wrong impression about you. Say what you have to say in a kind and gentle manner, then you will be able to win people over and inspire them. Moreover, worry and distress lead to backbiting about others and putting them down, which takes away reward, brings you a burden of sin and destroys tranquility. So, pay attention to correcting your own faults and forget about people's faults, for Allah did not create us perfect and infallible; rather, we all have sins and faults. So, glad tidings are to the one who focuses on dealing with his own faults rather than the faults of others.

"The mother whose child falls from a high place should not waste time weeping; rather, she should focus on tending to his injuries."

"Understand that whatever befalls
you could not have missed you." (Hadith)

8

Be cheerful at heart and the universe will embrace you

Look at life with a spirit of love and optimism, for life is a
gift from Allah to man. So accept this gift from the One, take it
with joy and embrace the morning with its glow and the night with
its quietness, and the day with its brightness. Drink this fresh
water with gratitude, breathe the fresh air with joy, smell the roses
and glorify Allah. Think about the universe and learn from it,
make use of the blessed gift of land, the beautiful flowers, the
sweet air, the delights of the garden, the warmth of the sun, the
light of the moon. Let these blessings motivate you to obey Allah,
the Exalted, give thanks to Him and praise Him for His blessings
and bounty. Do not let worry and distress prevent you from seeing
these blessings or make you ungrateful; rather, remember that the
Creator and Provider has only created these blessings as a means
to help you obey Him, and He says:

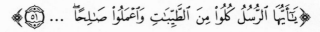

(سورة المؤمنون: ٥١)

❴O' [you] Messengers! Eat of the *Ṭayyibāt* [all kinds
of *Ḥalāl* (lawful) foods which Allah has made lawful
(meat of slaughtered eatable animals, milk products,
fats, vegetables, fruits)] and do righteous deeds...❵

(Qur'an 23: 51)

"The most sincere generosity comes from those who do not have anything but recognize the value of a kind word and a smile.
How many people give, but it is as if they are giving a slap."

❴... And whosoever fears Allah and keeps
his duty to Him, He will make a way
for him to get out [of every difficulty].❵

(Qur'an 65: 2)

9
No one is ever completely happy

You are making a big mistake if you think that life must always be one hundred percent in your favour. This is something that will only happen in Paradise. In this world, however, happiness is relative. You will not get everything you want; there will always be some problems, sickness, adversity and trials. So, be grateful at times of ease and patient at times of hardship. Do not be too idealistic and expect good health with no sickness, richness with no poverty, happiness with nothing to spoil your joy, a husband with no negative aspects, a friend with no faults. That will never happen. Learn how to overlook the negative aspects and mistakes, and look at the positive aspects and good things. Think well of others and make excuses for them, but put your trust in Allah only, because people are not fit to be relied upon or to have your affairs delegated to them:

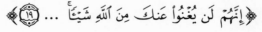

(سورة الجَاثِيَة: ١٩)

❴Verily, they can avail you nothing against Allah [if He wants to punish you...]...❵   *(Qur'an 45: 19)*

"Do not be content to have some dark areas in your life, for the light is there; all you have to do is to turn it on and see it shining."

❴... And whosoever fears Allah and keeps his duty
to Him, He will make his matter easy for him.❵

(Qur'an 65: 4)

10
Enter the garden of knowledge

One of the means of finding happiness is understanding
Islam, for learning about Islam brings contentment and pleases the
Lord. As the Prophet (Blessings and Peace be upon him) said:
*"When Allah intends good for a person, He grants him under-
standing of religion."* So read easily-available books of knowledge which will benefit you and increase you in knowledge and
understanding of Islam, such as *Riyāḍ aṣ-Ṣāliḥīn, Fiqh aṣ-
Sunnah, Fiqh ad-Dalīl,* easy *Tafsīrs* (Interpretations) and useful
essays. Remember that the best of your deeds is to know what
Allah meant in His Book and what the Prophet (Blessings and
Peace be upon him) meant in his Sunnah, so study the Qur'an a
great deal with your sisters, memorize whatever you can of it,
listen to and act upon it, because ignorance of Islam leads to
darkness and anxiety in the heart. You should have a home library,
even if it is small, containing useful books and tapes. Beware of
wasting time listening to songs and watching soap operas, for you
will be called to account for every second of your life, so make the
most of your time to please Allah, the Exalted, Almighty.

"The most difficult time could be
made easier by the smile of a
confident person."

Chapter 5

Chapter 5

❮... It may be that Allah will afterward
bring some new thing to pass.❯

1
Remember the shed tears and broken hearts

One of the literati said:

If you believe that you have a covenant with time such that things will only be the way you want in all your affairs, and you will only be given what you want and desire, then it makes sense to give yourself free rein to grieve every time you do not get what you want or when obstacles come between you and your goal. But if you are aware that things alternate, sometimes you get what you want and sometimes you miss out, and that life never gives you a gift and then forgets about it, rather it will come to take it back, and that this is the way life is for all the sons of Ādam, whether they live in palaces or hovels, for the one whose limit is the sky and the one who sleeps on the bare ground. So try to calm your grief and wipe away your tears, for you are not the only one stricken with calamities and your problems are nothing new or unjust in the annals of calamity and grief.

"Stop regretting your sin and think about the good deeds with which you are going to replace it."

"Calamities make people call upon Allah."

2
These people are not happy

Do not look at those who are living a life of luxury and extravagance, for they are to be pitied, not envied. People whose only concern is to spend extravagantly on themselves and indulge in their every whim and desire and seek pleasure — whether it is permissible or forbidden — are not happy. Rather, they are living a hard life of stress and worry, because no one who deviates from the path of Allah and disobeys Him will ever find happiness. So, do not think that those who live a life of luxury and extravagance are happy and content, not at all. Some poor women living in mud huts are better off than those who sleep on feather beds and sheets of brocade and silk in lofty palaces, because the poor woman who believes in Allah, the Exalted, and worships Him is better off than the one who has gone astray from the path of Allah.

> "Happiness exists in you and you should focus your efforts on yourself."

❨So know [O' Muhammad] that *Lā ilāha illa Allah*

[none has the right to be worshipped but Allah]...❩

(Qur'an 47: 19)

3
The way to Allah is the best way

What is happiness? Is happiness to be found in money or status or lineage? There are many answers, but let us look at the happiness of this woman:

A man had an argument with his wife and said, "I am going to make your life miserable." The wife calmly replied, "You cannot do that." He said, "Why not?" She said: "If happiness were to be found in money or jewellery, you could deprive me of it and take it away from me, but it is nothing over which you or any other person has any control. I find my happiness in my faith, and my faith is in my heart, and no one has any power over it except my Lord."

This is true happiness, the happiness of faith, and no one can feel this happiness except the one whose mind, heart and soul are filled with the love of Allah. The one who truly has control over happiness is the One True God, so seek happiness from Him by worshipping and obeying Him.

The only way to find happiness is by learning the true religion with which the Messenger of Allah (Blessings and Peace be upon him) was sent. Once a person finds this way, it will not matter if he sleeps in a hut or by the side of the road, and he will be content with a piece of bread, and he will be the happiest person in the world. But whoever goes astray from this path will find that his whole life is filled with grief, his wealth is deprivation, his efforts are loss and his end will be humiliation.

> "We need money in order to live but that does not mean that we need to live for the sake of money."

"O' Allah, I ask You for forgiveness and well-being."

4
When things become unbearable, turn to Allah

Ibn al-Jawzi said:

"Something was causing me a great deal of grief and distress, and I started to think long and hard about how to get out of this situation by any means, but I could not find any way out. Then I came across this verse:

$$ ﴾ ... وَمَن يَتَّقِ ٱللَّهَ يَجْعَل لَّهُۥ مَخْرَجًا ﴿٢﴾ ﴿   (سورة الطَّلَاق : ٢) $$

﴾... And whosoever fears Allah and keeps his duty to Him, He will make a way for him to get out [of every difficulty].﴿   *(Qur'an 65: 2)*

I realized that *taqwā* (piety, fearing Allah) is the way out of every kind of grief and distress. As soon as I followed the path of *taqwā*, I found the way out."

I say: for the wise men, *taqwā* is the way that leads to everything good, for calamity happens only as the result of sin, and it can only be lifted through repentance. Sadness, grief and worry are punishments for sins that you have committed, by falling short in your prayers, or backbiting about a Muslimah, or taking the matter of *ḥijāb* lightly, or committing a *ḥarām* (forbidden) action. Whoever goes against the laws of Allah, the Almighty, has to pay the price for that shortcoming. The One Who created happiness is the Most Gracious, Most Merciful, so how can you seek happiness from anyone other than Him? If people had control over happiness, there would be no deprived or grieving person left on earth.

> **"Cast away all discouraging thoughts that make you feel helpless, and focus on success, then you will never fail."**

"I am as My servant thinks I am."   *(Hadith qudsi)*

5
Make every day a new beginning

Staying away from Allah, the Exalted, only bears bitter fruit, and the gifts of intelligence, strength, beauty and knowledge will all turn to calamity and loss if they are kept away from the guidance of Allah, the Exalted, and deprived of His blessings. Hence, Allah has warned people of the consequences of staying away from Him.

If you are walking down the street and a car comes towards you at high speed and you feel it will hit you and kill you, you have no choice but to act quickly and try to get away... Allah wants to warn His slaves that they face a similar kind of destruction if they turn away from Him, so He urges them to seek safety with Him alone:

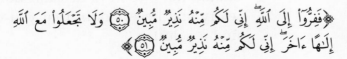

(سورة الذَّارِيَات : ٥٠-٥١)

❨So flee to Allah [from His Torment to His Mercy — Islamic Monotheism]. Verily, I [Muhammad] am a plain warner to you from Him. And set not up [or worship not] any other *ilāh* [god] along with Allah [Glorified be He (Alone), Exalted above all that they associate as partners with Him]. Verily, I [Muhammad] am a plain warner to you from Him.❩

(Qur'an 51: 50-51)

Turning to Allah requires a person to renew himself, reorganize his life, develop a better relationship with his Lord, and do better deeds. It is the start of a new covenant that is summed up in the following *du'ā'*:

"Allahumma anta rabbi lā ilāha illā anta. Khalaqtani wa ana 'abduka wa ana 'ala 'ahdika wa wa'dika ma istaṭa'tu. A'ūdhu bika min sharri ma ṣana'ta. Abū'u laka bi ni'matika 'alayya wa abū'u bi dhanbi faghfir li fa innahu lā yaghfiru adh-dhunūba illā anta.

[O' Allah, You are my Lord and there is no god but You. You created me and I am Your slave. And I am trying my best to keep my oath (of faith) to You and to live in the hope of Your promise. I seek refuge in You from my greatest evil-deeds. I acknowledge Your blessings upon me and I acknowledge my sins. So forgive me, for none but You can forgive sins']."

"If you fail in one of your deeds, you should not give in to despair; do not worry and never doubt that you will find a solution."

"Your smiling at your sister is (an act of) charity."

6
Women are like stars in the sky

The righteous Muslim woman is the one who treats her husband kindly and obeys him after obeying her Lord. The Messenger of Allah (Blessings and Peace be upon him) praised such women and regarded them as the ideal wives that men should look for. When the Prophet (Blessings and Peace be upon him) was asked which woman is best, he said: *"The one who makes him (her husband) happy when he looks at her, who obeys him when he tells her to do something, and who does not oppose him in a manner that he dislikes with regard to herself or his wealth."*

When Allah, the Exalted, revealed the words,

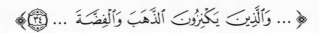

(سورة التوبة : ٣٤)

❴... And those who hoard up gold and silver [*al-Kanz*: the money, the *Zakāh* of which has not been paid]...❵

(Qur'an 9: 34)

'Umar went out, and Thawbān (may Allah be pleased with them) followed him. 'Umar came to the Prophet (Blessings and Peace be upon him) and said: "O' Prophet of Allah, this verse has made your Companions worried." The Prophet said: *"Shall I not tell you of something that is a man's treasure? A righteous woman who pleases him when he looks at her, when he tells her to do something, she obeys him, and if he is away from her, she is faithful."*

The Messenger of Allah (Blessings and Peace be upon him) stated that a woman's admission to Paradise depends on whether her husband is pleased with her. It was narrated that Umm Salamah (may Allah be pleased with her) said: "The Messenger of Allah said: *'Any woman who dies when her husband is pleased with her, will enter Paradise.'*" So be such a woman and you will be happy.

"There is room for you in the first row, provided you do your best to be profi-cient in all that you do."

"Be happy just to be alive."

7

Death is preferable to doing <u>harām</u> (forbidden) actions

According to the hadith narrated by 'Abdullāh ibn 'Umar ibn al-Khaṭṭāb (may Allah be pleased with him) about the three people who stayed overnight in the cave, then a rock fell down the mountain and blocked the entrance of the cave, so they prayed to Allah, the Exalted, to save them and mentioned their righteous deeds, the second of them said:

"O' Allah, I had a female cousin who was the most beloved of people to me — according to another report, I used to love her as much as any man can love a woman — and I approached her but she refused my approaches, until in one year she became very poor and desperate, so she came to me and I gave her one hundred and twenty *dinars* on condition that she lets me have my way with her. But when I sat between her legs she said, 'Fear Allah, and do not tear it apart except in a lawful manner.' This girl was pious and did not let him have his way with her initially, but when she was in desperate need because of poverty, she had no choice, but she reminded him of Allah, the Powerful, and told him to fear Him. This prompted feelings of faith in his heart and reminded him that if he wanted her, he should marry her in a proper manner and not commit *zinā* (adultery) with her. That deterred him and he repented to Allah, the Almighty, Most Merciful, and that was the cause that part of the rock was moved on the day it blocked the door of the cave.

"Learn how to co-exist with fear and it will disappear."

"Your life is the product of your thoughts."

8
Inspiring verses

Allah, the Exalted, says:

﴿ ... فَلْيُنْفِقْ مِمَّا ءَاتَنهُ ٱللَّهُ ... ٧ ﴾   (سورة الطَّلاق : ٧)

﴿... After hardship, Allah will create ease.﴾
(Qur'an 65: 7)

﴿يَتَأَيُّهَا ٱلَّذِينَ ءَامَنُوا۟ ٱصْبِرُوا۟ وَصَابِرُوا۟ وَرَابِطُوا۟ وَٱتَّقُوا۟ ٱللَّهَ لَعَلَّكُمْ تُفْلِحُونَ ٢٠٠ ﴾   (سورة آل عِمْرَان : ٢٠٠)

﴿O' you who have believed, persevere and endure and remain stationed and fear Allah that you may be successful.﴾
(Qur'an 3: 200)

﴿ ... وَبَشِّرِ ٱلصَّبِرِينَ ١٥٥ ٱلَّذِينَ إِذَآ أَصَبَتْهُم مُّصِيبَةٌ قَالُوٓا۟ إِنَّا لِلَّهِ وَإِنَّآ إِلَيْهِ رَجِعُونَ ١٥٦ ﴾   (سورة البَقَرَة : ١٥٥–١٥٦)

﴿... But give glad tidings to *aṣ-Ṣābirīn* [the patient]. Who, when afflicted with calamity, say: 'Truly, to Allah we belong and truly, to Him we shall return.'﴾
(Qur'an 2: 155-156)

﴿وَهُوَ ٱلَّذِى يُنَزِّلُ ٱلْغَيْثَ مِنۢ بَعْدِ مَا قَنَطُوا۟ وَيَنشُرُ رَحْمَتَهُ ... ٢٨ ﴾   (سورة الشُّورىٰ : ٢٨)

﴿And He it is Who sends down the rain after they have despaired, and spreads His Mercy...﴾
(Qur'an 42: 28)

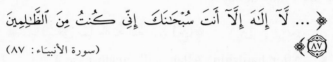

﴾ ... تَشْكُرُوا وَإِن ٱلْكُفْرَ وَازِرَةٌ تَزِرُ وَلَا ۝ ﴿

(سورة الزُّمَر: ١٠)

﴾... Only those who are patient shall receive their reward in full, without reckoning.﴿ *(Qur'an 39: 10)*

And Allah tells us that *Dhu an-Nūn* called out:

﴾ ... لَّآ إِلَٰهَ إِلَّآ أَنتَ سُبْحَٰنَكَ إِنِّى كُنتُ مِنَ ٱلظَّٰلِمِينَ ۝ ﴿

(سورة الأنبيَاء: ٨٧)

﴾... *Lā ilāha illa Anta* [none has the right to be worshipped but You (O' Allah)], Glorified [and Exalted] be You [above all that (evil) they associate with You]! Truly, I have been of the wrongdoers.﴿

(Qur'an 21: 87)

The Qur'an calls you to be happy and rest assured, and to trust your Lord, and open your heart to the true promise of Allah. For He has not created mankind to torment them, rather, He has created them to test them, purify them and discipline them. Allah is more compassionate and merciful to a person than his father and mother. So seek mercy, comfort and pleasure from Him — may He be exalted and glorified — by remembering Him, giving thanks to Him, reading His Book and following His Messenger (Blessings and Peace be upon him).

> "Prepare for the worst, then you will feel that things are getting better."

*"It is sufficient honour for women that the
mother of Muhammad (Blessings and Peace
be upon him) was a woman."*

9
Knowledge of the Most Merciful takes away grief

Allah, the Most Generous, Most Kind, gives to His slave
more than he can hope for before he even asks. He appreciates
small deeds and makes them grow, and He forgives and erases a
great deal of mistakes.

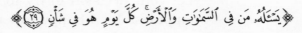

(سورة الرَّحمٰن: ٢٩)

❝Whosoever in the heavens and on earth asks Him.
Every day He is [engaged] in some affair [such as
giving honour or disgrace to some, life or death to
some]!❞   *(Qur'an 55: 29)*

He is not distracted and He listens to all; He does not get confused
by being asked for so many things; He does not tire when people
persist in calling upon Him. Rather, He loves them to persist in
calling upon Him and He likes to be asked; He gets angry when
He is not asked. He is kind to His slave when His slave does not
care about Him; He conceals His slave when His slave does not
conceal himself; He shows mercy to His slave when His slave
does not show mercy to himself. How can hearts not love Him
when no one guides them to do good deeds but Him, when no one

takes away evil deeds but Him, when no one answers prayers, forgives errors, conceals faults, relieves distress, comes to the aid of the desperate and grants blessings and mercy except Him?

Allah, the Exalted ... the Most Bountiful of those who give, the Most Merciful of those who are asked for mercy, the Most Generous of those whose help is sought, the Most Powerful of those to whom people turn, the most caring of those in whom people put their trust. He is more merciful to His slave than a mother to her child, and He rejoices more at the repentance of His slave than one who lost his mount on which is his food and drink in a barren land, then when he has despaired and thinks he is about to die, he finds it.

> "Let your decision to try to achieve happiness be a happy experience in and of itself."

《And Allah has set forth an example for those who believe: the wife of Fir'awn [Pharaoh]...》

(Qur'an 66: 11)

10
The blessed day

Try, when you pray *Fajr*, to sit in a humble manner and face the *qiblah* for ten or fifteen minutes, remembering Allah a great deal and calling upon Him. Ask Allah for a good day, a blessed day, a happy day, a day of success and achievement with no calamities, crises or problems, a day with bountiful provision, goodness and care. A day with no distress or worry — because from Allah one may ask for happiness, provision and all that is good. If you sit like this and pray, this will — by Allah's leave — be guaranteed to prepare you for a good, blessed and useful day.

If you have work to do or you are simply sitting, it is advisable to listen to a little Qur'an from a tape or the radio, from a humble reader with a fine voice, so you can listen to the verses of Allah from His Book, and focus with proper humility whilst listening, thus washing away any doubt and distress that may be in your heart, and making you better than you were before.

"Do not worry about things that you cannot perform, rather, spend time on improving what you can improve."

Chapter 6

Chapter 6

⟪... Yes! Certainly, the Help of Allah is near!⟫

(Qur'an 2: 214)

1

A wise woman is the source of a happy life

A woman should welcome her husband warmly when he comes back to her; she should not get upset if she finds him stressed and tired. On the contrary, she should rush to fulfil his requests no matter what they are, without asking him the reason for his being stressed and tired as soon as he comes home. Once he has changed his clothes and settled down, he may soon tell her why he is feeling stressed, and if he does not, there is nothing wrong with her asking him, but she should ask in a way that makes him feel that she is concerned about him and cares for him, and is worried about the state in which he came home.

If the wife finds that she is able to help her husband to solve the problem that caused him stress, then she should hasten to do so. If she does that, it will lighten the load for her husband a great deal, and the husband will feel that in his home there is a precious jewel, one that is even more precious than all the jewels in the world.

"Do not feel sad or miserable because of some work that you could not complete, rather you should understand that the work of great people is never done."

"When Allah loves some people He tests them."

(Hadith)

2

Take care of today only

A happy person once said:

"The beautiful day is the day on which we have control of our affairs and our affairs do not control us. It is the day on which we control our desires and we are not controlled by them like slaves.

Some of these days I can remember and will never forget.

Every day on which I managed to save myself from the vicious circle of worrying about what I can and cannot do is a wonderful day.

How wonderful is the day on which I was hesitating whether to do a deed for which people would praise me or a deed for which no one would praise me, and no one would know about it, so I forsook the praise of people and was content to do an action which I will remember for as long as I live, but which no one will hear about.

How wonderful is the day on which I felt that my pockets were filling with money but my conscience was devoid of dignity, so I decided that I would rather be penniless and have a clear conscience.

These days are wonderful, and the most wonderful thing about them is that my worldly gain on these days is very small, but the fact that I gained self-respect from my actions far outweighs that, and what I gained on such days is great, praise be to Allah, the Exalted, All-Merciful."

"Be happy with what is in your hand,
content with whatever Allah has
decreed and give up all daydreams
that do not suit your efforts and
abilities."

❨... Allah has forgiven what is past...❩

(Qur'an 5: 95)

3
Do not feel that everyone is out to get you

This is an important principle that will help you to overcome anxiety, succeed in life in general, keep your friends and be happy with your family, because the one who has deep insight understands the nature of people and how things may change; he puts himself in the other person's shoes and understands situations both obvious and hidden.

With regard to anxiety itself, the person who has deep insight understands realities, and knows that when he is faced with a problem or when things do not turn out the way he wanted, that this is life and that no one is totally content with his lot; a person may dislike something that is good for him, or he may delight in something that is bad for him, and goodness is to be found in that which Allah, the Exalted, decrees.

The person who has deep insight feels that he is part of this great universe, and that he will have a share of pain and grief, but also of happiness. He does not get taken unaware by things, nor does he feel that he is the only one who is suffering as does the one who has little insight, who thinks that he is the only one who is faced with this problem, or that people are out to get him, or that he always has bad luck. The one who has deep insight does not feel any such thing, rather, he understands the way life is, and he knows that he is a part of it, so he accepts it after doing his utmost to do what is best.

> **"Be happy now, today, not tomorrow."**

❲*Salāmun 'Alaykum* [peace be upon you]

for you persevered in patience!...❳

(Qur'an 13: 24)

4
How sweet is success after hardship

A successful person said:

"I was born poor and poverty stayed with me from the cradle. I knew the bitterness of asking my mother for a piece of bread when she could not even find a piece of dry crust to give me. I left home when I was ten years old and started to work when I was eleven. I studied for only one month of every year. After eleven years of hard work I acquired a pair of oxen and six sheep which earned me eighty-four dollars. I never spent a single penny in my life on pleasure; rather, I used to save every penny I earned from the day I grew up until I reached the age of twenty-one. I knew what real exhaustion was, and I travelled for miles to ask my fellow men to let me do some work so that I could earn a living. In the first month after I reached the age of twenty-one, I went to the forest, driving a cart pulled by the two oxen to cut firewood. I used to get up before dawn every day and I would continue working hard until darkness fell, just to get six dollars at the end of the month, and each one of those dollars looked to me like a full moon on a dark night."

"If you have made mistakes in the past, learn from them, then let them go."

❰Say [O' Muhammad]: "Allah rescues you from
this and from all [other] distresses"...❱

(Qur'an 6: 64)

5

You will adapt to your situation and cope with it

I know a man who had his foot amputated, so I went to console him. He was a wise and knowledgeable man, and I wanted to tell him:

"The *ummah* (nation) does not expect you to be a fast runner or a champion wrestler; rather, it expects you to offer wise opinions and enlightened thoughts, and you still have that, praise be to Allah, the Exalted."

When I visited him, he said to me:

"Praise be to Allah, this foot of mine stayed with me for decades, and it was a good companion. But my religious commitment is what comforts me."

A wise man said:

"Peace of mind can only be acquired by accepting the worst-case scenario."

The reason for that, from a psychological point of view, is that acceptance releases energy. But in spite of that, thousands upon thousands of people destroy their lives in a moment of anger, because they refuse to accept the bitter reality and save whatever can be saved, instead of trying to build up their hopes from scratch and indulging in a bitter fight with the past, so they give in to that anxiety that serves no purpose.

According to the Islamic viewpoint, regretting past failures and weeping bitterly for past pain and defeat are manifestations of disbelief in Allah, the Almighty, and discontent with what He has decreed.

> "Frustration is your worst enemy, for it has the power to destroy peace of mind."

❪Thus We have made you a just [and the best] nation...❫

(Qur'an 2: 143)

6

Sound advice from a wise woman

There is concise advice which is among the best advice narrated from Arab women. This is the advice given by Umāmah bint al-Ḥārith to her daughter Umm Iyās bint 'Awf on the night of her wedding. Among the advice she offered was the following:

"O' my daughter! You are about to leave the home in which you grew up, where you first learned to walk, to go to a place you do not know, to a companion with whom you are unfamiliar. By marrying you, he has become a master over you, so be like a servant to him, and he will become like a servant to you.

Take from me ten qualities, which will be a provision and a reminder for you:

The first and second of them are: Be content in his company, and listen to and obey him, for contentment brings peace of mind, and listening to and obeying one's husband pleases Allah, the All-Glorious, All-Merciful.

The third and fourth of them are: Make sure that you smell good and look good; he should not see anything ugly in you, and he should not smell anything but a pleasant smell from you.

The fifth and the sixth of them are: Prepare his food on time, and keep quiet when he is asleep, for raging hunger is like a burning flame, and disturbing his sleep will make him angry.

The seventh and eighth of them are: take care of his servants (or employees) and children, and take care of his wealth, for taking care of his wealth shows that you appreciate him, and taking care of his children and servants shows good management.

The ninth and tenth of them are: never disclose any of his secrets, and never disobey any of his orders, for if you disclose any of his secrets you will never feel safe from his possible betrayal, and if you disobey him, his heart will be filled with hatred towards you.

Be careful, O' my daughter, of showing joy in front of him when he is upset, and do not show sorrow in front of him when he is happy."

> "Your happiness does not depend on anyone else, rather, it is in your hands."

"Tomorrow the sun will rise and gladden your heart."

7
A woman who offered herself as a sacrifice and thus earned the pleasure of her Lord

Have you heard of the Juhani woman who made a mistake and committed *zinā* (fornication), then she remembered Allah and turned to Him in repentance, and she came to the Messenger of Allah (Blessings and Peace be upon him) wanting him to stone her and purify her? She came pregnant as a result of *zinā*, and said, "O' Messenger of Allah, I have committed a sin that deserves a *ḥadd* (legal punishment), so carry out the punishment on me." The Prophet (Blessings and Peace be upon him) called her guardian and said: "Treat her kindly, then when she gives birth come to me." He did that, then the Prophet ordered that her clothes be tied tightly around her, then he ordered that she be stoned. Then he offered the funeral prayer for her. 'Umar said to him: "O' Messenger of Allah, are you praying for her when she has committed *zinā*?" He (Blessings and Peace be upon him) said: *"She has repented in such a way that if it were shared among seventy of the people of Madīnah, it would be sufficient for them. Can you find any better than one who sacrificed herself for the sake of Allah?"*

It was strong faith that motivated her to seek purification and to choose the Hereafter over this world. If she had not had such strong faith, she would not have preferred death by stoning.

Someone might object by saying, Why did she commit *zinā*? Wasn't that no more than the result of weak faith? The answer is that a person may become weak and make a mistake, because he was created from weakness, and he may slip because he is created of haste *(cf. Qur'an 21: 37)*, and he may go astray for a brief moment because he is imperfect. But when the seed of faith grows in his heart and bears fruit, his good essence and strong faith will be made manifest. This is what made this woman rush to the Messenger of Allah (Blessings and Peace be upon him) and ask him to purify her, so she sacrificed herself in pursuit of the pleasure, mercy and forgiveness of Allah.

> "Do not be a chronic complainer, or
> an amateur complainer!"

"The night is darkest just before the dawn."

8
She adhered to the commands of Allah and Allah protected her

The story is told of a beautiful and wealthy woman who lingered in her house with her slaves and did not flee when the Crusaders attacked Alexandria. The Franks entered her house with drawn swords in their hands, and one of them said to her, "Where is the money?"

She said, terrified: "The money is in these trunks in this room," and she pointed towards the trunks which were in the room where she was sitting. She started to tremble with fear. One of them said, "Do not be afraid, for you will be with me, and you will enjoy my wealth and my kindness." She understood that he liked her and wanted her for himself.. So she leaned towards him and said, "I want to go to the lavatory," " and she spoke to him softly and kindly.

He thought that she also wanted him, so he gestured to her that she should go and relieve herself, so she want away and they started to take the trunks away. The woman went out of her house into a storeroom filled with straw, and buried herself in it. The Franks looked for her, after plundering her house, but they could not find her, so they carried away the plunder and left. The woman managed to escape being taken prisoner by means of this trick, and her slaves also managed to escape capture by hiding on the roof of the house.

The woman said: "Saving my religious commitment and honour is better than wealth and jewels which are kept by chivalrous men for only such a purpose (i.e., to ensure the soundness of their religious commitment and honour), because being poor is better than being a prisoner and compelled to change one's religion by force."

"You have to accept the inescapable fact, which is that you will encounter things in life that you cannot change, but you can deal with through patience and faith."

"A mother is the producer of men and heroes."

9
The water of repentance is the purest water

Allah loves those who repent, and He loves those who purify themselves. He rejoices over the repentance of His slave more than a man rejoices when he finds his mount which carries his food and drink, after losing it in a barren land falling into despair and sitting by the root of a tree to await death, then he suddenly sees his animal standing by his head, with his food and drink on it, so he gets up and takes hold of its reins, and cries out in joy, "O' Allah, You are my Lord and I am your slave!" Glory be to Allah, how great He is and how merciful, for He rejoices at His slave's repentance and his attaining Paradise and earning His pleasure. Allah calls His believing slaves with the words:

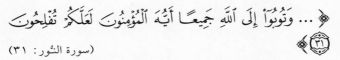

(سورة النُّور: ٣١)

❲... And turn to Allah in repentance, all of you, O' believers, that you may be successful.❳

(Qur'an 24: 31)

Repentance cleanses the heart with the water of tears and the fire of regret which burns in the heart, and with a feeling of humility and tears in the eyes. This is the first step of those who seek a path to Allah, it is the capital of those who are successful, and the key to correcting those who have gone astray. The one who repents prays to Allah and beseeches Him, weeping. When others relax he does not, when others are still his fear does not rest and the longing of his heart never ceases. He stands before his Lord with a grieving heart and distressed mind, bowing his head and trembling when he remembers how many sins he committed. His grief overwhelms him and his tears flow. He prepares himself to be a winner tomorrow and to shed his worldly load so that he may pass quickly over the bridge of Hell.

"Think positively when things get bad on one day, for that may be the prelude to another day filled with joy and happiness."

❨... And guard in the husband's absence what
Allah orders them to guard [e.g. their chastity and their
husband's property].❩ *(Qur'an 4: 34)*

10
The first freedom fighter

She lived in the greatest palace of her time, with many
slaves, male and female at her command. Hers was a life of luxury
and ease.

Her name was Āsiyah bint Muzāḥim, the wife of Pharaoh
— may Allah be pleased with her — one woman, physically
weak, but she was a believer who was at peace in her palace. The
light of faith had dawned in her heart and she challenged the
system of *jāhiliyah* (ignorance) at the head of which was her
husband.

She had deep insight and did not care about palaces and
luxurious furnishings or having many slaves and servants. Hence,
she deserved to be mentioned by the Lord of the Worlds in His
Holy Book, where she is given as an example for those who
believe, as Allah, the Exalted, says:

﴿وَضَرَبَ ٱللَّهُ مَثَلًا لِّلَّذِينَ ءَامَنُواْ ٱمْرَأَتَ فِرْعَوْنَ إِذْ قَالَتْ رَبِّ
ٱبْنِ لِي عِندَكَ بَيْتًا فِي ٱلْجَنَّةِ وَنَجِّنِي مِن فِرْعَوْنَ وَعَمَلِهِۦ وَنَجِّنِي
مِنَ ٱلْقَوْمِ ٱلظَّٰلِمِينَ ﴿١١﴾﴾ (سورة التحريم: ١١)

❨And Allah has set forth an example for those who
believe: the wife of Fir'awn [Pharaoh], when she
said: "My Lord! Build for me a home with You in

Paradise, and save me from Fir'awn [Pharaoh] and his work, and save me from the people who are *Zālimūn* [polytheists, wrongdoers and disbelievers in Allah].❭   *(Qur'an 66: 11)*

The scholars said, commenting on this verse:

Āsiyah chose the Hereafter over this world. She also deserved to be mentioned by the Prophet (Blessings and Peace be upon him) among the perfect women, when he said: *"Many men attain perfection but no women attained perfection except Āsiyah the wife of Pharaoh and Maryam bint 'Imrān, and the superiority of 'Ā'ishah over other women is like the superiority of tharīd (bread, meat and broth) over other foods."*

This is Āsiyah the believer, the lamp that shone in the darkness of Pharaoh's palace. Who could light a lamp for us that shines with such patience and steadfastness, calling us to Allah, the Almighty?

> **"Control your thoughts and you will be happy."**

Chapter 7

❴... Surely, Allah's Mercy is [ever] near
unto the good-doers.❵

(Qur'an 7: 56)

1
Put your trust in your Lord

To any woman who went asleep, satisfied with the decree of Allah despite a surrounding hurricane, untroubled by the turmoil around her, not allowing sorrow to enter her heart or tears to fall from her eyes; to any woman who has lost children, loved ones, parents and friends; to every distressed believer, and to everyone who is faced with calamities and trials:

May Allah, the Almighty, increase your reward, raise you in status and compensate your loss. Allah, the Exalted, says:

﴿وَٱسْتَعِينُوا۟ بِٱلصَّبْرِ وَٱلصَّلَوٰةِ ۚ وَإِنَّهَا لَكَبِيرَةٌ إِلَّا عَلَى ٱلْخَٰشِعِينَ ٤٥﴾

(سورة البَقَرَة: ٤٥)

❴And seek help through patience and *aṣ-Ṣalāh* [prayer], and truly it is extremely heavy and hard except for *al-Khāshi'īn* [i.e. the true believers in Allah — those who obey Allah with full submission, fear much of His punishment, and believe in His Promise (Paradise) and in His Warnings (Hell)].❵

(Qur'an 2: 45)

'Ali (may Allah be pleased with him) said:

"The relation of patience to faith is like that of the head to the body."

— Rejoice in the glad tidings of the Hereafter, a place in *Firdaws* close to the One, in *Jannāt ‘Adan* (the Garden of Eden), in a seat of truth *(cf. Qur'an 54: 55)*, as a reward for what you sent on ahead and for your efforts and giving. Congratulations for your faith, patience and hope of reward; you will come to know that you will succeed in all situations:

﴿ ... وَبَشِّرِ ٱلصَّٰبِرِينَ ﴾ (سورة البَقَرَة: ١٥٥)

﴿... but give glad tidings to *aṣ-Ṣābirīn* [the patient].﴾
(Qur'an 2: 155)

"Self-confidence means finding
meaning in life regardless of your
age; and being able to gain more
from life."

❨Allah is very Gracious and
Kind to His slaves...❩

(Qur'an 42: 19)

2
Blindness of the heart is real blindness

There was a blind man who lived happily with his loving wife, his devoted son and his good friend. The only thing that bothered him was the darkness in which he lived. He wished that he could see the light and the things that made him happy with his own eyes.

A brilliant doctor came to the city in which this blind man lived, so he went to him and asked him for medicine that would help him to see. The doctor gave him some drops and told him how to use them, and warned him that he may see suddenly, at any moment.

The blind man continued to use the drops even though no one else believed that they would work, but after a few days he saw the light suddenly, whilst sitting in his garden. He was filled with joy and ran into the house to tell his dear wife, but he saw her in his room, betraying him with his friend, and he could not believe what he saw. Then he went to the other room and saw his son stealing something from his cupboard.

The blind man retraced his steps, screaming,

"This is not a doctor, this is an accursed sorcerer!"

Then he took a pin and pierced his eyes, and nervously went back to the happiness that he was used to.[1]

"Psychological anxiety is worse than physical illnesses."

---

[1] The moral of this sad tale is that we should accept the lot that we have been given in life, with whatever limitations have been decreed for us, because as the saying goes, the grass isn't always greener on the other side. (Translator)

❨... Nay, verily, with me is my Lord. He will guide me.❩

(Qur'an 26: 62)

3
Do not try to establish a court of vengeance, for you may be the first victim

Some people are easy going and do not care about settling scores or taking all their dues in full; they overlook many things and may even play dumb sometimes, but in general they are easy-going, pleasant and do not examine things thoroughly or try to read between the lines. They do not worry about such things.

Others do not know the meaning of tolerance nor overlook the slightest thing. They are engaged in a constant battle with other people to get their dues in full.

Naturally, the one who is tolerant is more likely to be content, calm and free of anxiety, and more deserving of people's love and affection. The door of success is more likely to be open to him than many of those who think of themselves as being in a constant battle with people, and who analyze all words and situations, looking for evil intentions. Such persons bring anxiety upon themselves in all ways, and people hate them and try to avoid them. The doors of success are closed to them. The Messenger of Allah (Blessings and Peace be upon him) was never given the choice between two things but he chose that which was easier, unless it was a sin, in which case he would be the most stringent of people in keeping away from it.

The Messenger of Allah (Blessings and Peace be upon him) said: *"May Allah have mercy on one who is easy-going when he sells, easy-going when he buys, and easy-going when he asks for his dues from people."*

"You should do what you can now, and do not worry about what tomorrow will bring."

❁We have not sent down the Qur'an unto you
[O' Muhammad] to cause you distress.❁

(Qur'an 20: 2)

4
Distinction is earned by achievement

A rich man said:

I have no special feelings about being the richest man in the world. I live an ordinary life in a modest apartment with my wife. I do not drink or smoke and I do not like the billionaire lifestyle as depicted in the newspapers, with luxury yachts, mansions in country sides, noisy parties and marriages to beautiful girls, which usually end in divorce with settlements costing millions of dollars.

I like working and I am happy to work. I usually take my lunch with me to eat it in the workplace. I do not feel happy when I think about all the millions I own. What makes me happy is when I remember how I helped to change my hometown of Tokyo from a humble town to a capital city that is the focal point of world attention with its modern architecture that I introduced... in brief, my happiness comes from my achievements.

"Regret cannot salvage a ship from the bottom of the sea."

❲Is not Allah Sufficient for His slave?...❳ *(Qur'an 39: 36)*

5
The world of kufr (disbelief) is suffering from misery

A doctor at the Mayo Clinic delivered a paper to the American Association of Physicians and Surgeons studying work in industrial institutions, in which he said that he studied 176 cases involving businessmen, all of whom were around the age of forty-four, and he found out that more than one-third of them were suffering from one of three diseases, all of which were the result of stress, namely heart problems, stomach ulcers and high blood pressure. All of these before any of them had reached the age of forty-five! Is a man to be considered successful if that is at the price of a stomach ulcer or heart trouble? What can it benefit a sick man if he gains the whole world but loses his health? Even if a man owns the whole world, he can only sleep on one bed, and he cannot eat more than three meals a day. What is the difference between him and a worker who digs the ground? The worker probably sleeps better and enjoys his food more than the man of high status and position.

Dr. W. S. Alvarez said: It is clear that four out of every five illnesses have no physical cause, rather the disease stems from fear, anxiety, hatred, selfishness and a person's inability to adapt to life.

"We cannot change the past or draw the future as we want. Why should we kill ourselves regretting something that we cannot change?"

"Do not get angry, do not get angry, do not get angry."

(Hadith)

6
The attitude of a life-partner

The righteous believing woman does not exhaust her husband with too many requests. She is content with which Allah has decreed for her. Her example in that is the family of the Messenger of Allah (Blessings and Peace be upon him). 'Urwah narrated from his maternal aunt 'Ā'ishah (may Allah be pleased with her) that she used to say: "By Allah, O' son of my brother! We watched the new moon come, then the next, then the next, three new moons in two months, and no fire was lit in the houses of the Messenger of Allah." I said: "O' aunt! What did you live on?" She said: "The two black ones, dates and water. But the Messenger of Allah had some neighbours among the *Anṣār*, (Madīnan Muslims who helped the Makkan Muslim migrants). They had goats, so they used to send some of their milk to the Messenger of Allah and he gave it to us to drink."

"The value of life is to live every minute of it."

"Work is the fuel of hope and the enemy of failure."

7
Be content with what
Allah has decreed for you

How beautiful are the words of Hājar (may Allah be pleased with her), the wife of Ibrāhīm and the mother of Ismāʿīl, when she followed her husband, after he had left her with her son in a valley that was not cultivated, and departed. She kept asking him, "O' Ibrāhīm! Where are you going and leaving us in this valley, where there are no people and nothing?" He did not answer her, so she said: "Has Allah commanded you to do this?" He said: "Yes." She said: "Then He will not forsake us." Indeed, Allah does not forsake His righteous slaves. Did not Allah compensate the man and his wife in *Sūrah al-Kahf*?

﴿وَأَمَّا ٱلْغُلَٰمُ فَكَانَ أَبَوَاهُ مُؤْمِنَيْنِ فَخَشِينَآ أَن يُرْهِقَهُمَا طُغْيَٰنًا
وَكُفْرًا ۝ فَأَرَدْنَآ أَن يُبْدِلَهُمَا رَبُّهُمَا خَيْرًا مِّنْهُ زَكَوٰةً وَأَقْرَبَ
رُحْمًا ۝﴾   (سورة الكهف: ٨٠–٨١)

﴿And as for the boy, his parents were believers, and
we feared that he would oppress them by rebellion
and disbelief. So we intended that their Lord should
change him for them for one better in righteousness
and nearer to mercy.﴾   *(Qur'an 18: 80-81)*

Did Allah not take care of the treasure of the righteous man for his two sons, when He commanded the companion of Mūsa to rebuild the wall so that it would remain strong until the two boys grew up and could take their father's treasure?

﴿وَأَمَّا ٱلْجِدَارُ فَكَانَ لِغُلَمَيْنِ يَتِيمَيْنِ فِى ٱلْمَدِينَةِ وَكَانَ تَحْتَهُ
كَنزٌ لَّهُمَا وَكَانَ أَبُوهُمَا صَلِحًا فَأَرَادَ رَبُّكَ أَن يَبْلُغَآ أَشُدَّهُمَا
وَيَسْتَخْرِجَا كَنزَهُمَا رَحْمَةً مِّن رَّبِّكَ ... ۝﴾

(سورة الكهف : ٨٢)

◆And as for the wall, it belonged to two orphan boys
in the town; and there was under it a treasure belong-
ing to them; and their father was a righteous man, and
your Lord intended that they should attain their age of
full strength and take out their treasure as a mercy
from your Lord...◆   *(Qur'an 18: 82)*

**"I cannot change the past nor know
what is to come, so why should I
regret anything or worry?"**

"Help comes with patience."

8
Do not feel any regret about this world

Whoever realizes how short this life is and how little joy there is in it, how unpredictable it is and how quickly things change for those whose main concern is this world, will not feel any regret for anything in it; they will never despair for whatever passes or feel sad about anything they have missed. For we have the Hereafter which is greater and more lasting, better than this world. So praise Allah, for you believe in the meeting with the One, whilst others — non-Muslim women — do not believe in that promised Day. Congratulations to those who believe in that Day and prepare for it. Doomed are those whose faith is weak and who forget about that Day, and get distracted by their palaces, houses, treasures and cheap luxuries. What value can there be in a palace or house or jewellery, if one has no faith? What worth can there be in status or position if you do not fear Allah? If power, position or wealth could buy happiness, why do we see so many kings, rulers and businessmen living miserable lives, complaining bitterly about their misfortunes?

"Yesterday is a dream that has gone and tomorrow is merely a beautiful hope. Only today is real."

"Women have produced the great men of this world."

9

The most wondrous beauty lies in the creation of Allah

Look at man and the marvelous way in which he is created, with his different races, languages, and accents. Allah, the Most High, has made him in the most beautiful form, as He says:

$$ ﴿ ... وَصَوَّرَكُمْ فَأَحْسَنَ صُوَرَكُمْ ... ﴾ $$

(سورة غَافِر: ٦٤)

﴾... And has given you shape and made your shapes good [looking]...﴿   *(Qur'an 40: 64)*

$$ ﴿يَٰٓأَيُّهَا ٱلْإِنسَٰنُ مَا غَرَّكَ بِرَبِّكَ ٱلْكَرِيمِ ٱلَّذِى خَلَقَكَ فَسَوَّىٰكَ فَعَدَلَكَ﴾ $$

[الانفِطار: ٦-٧]

﴾O' man! What has deceived you about your Lord, the Most Generous? Who created you, proportioned you, and balanced you?﴿   *(Qur'an 82: 6-7)*

$$ ﴿لَقَدْ خَلَقْنَا ٱلْإِنسَٰنَ فِىٓ أَحْسَنِ تَقْوِيمٍ﴾ $$ (سورة التِّين: ٤)

﴾Verily, We created man in the best stature [mould].﴿
(Qur'an 95: 4)

Look at the beauty of the sky and the stars, the splendour of the sun and the moon, the vastness of space. Look at the earth and how it is spread out, and its water and pasture are brought forth from it; look at the mountains and how they are fixed firmly.

Think about these seas and rivers, this night and day, this light and shade, these clouds. Think about how harmony exists throughout the universe. Look at these flowers, these ripe fruits, this delicious milk, this sweet honey, these palm trees, these bees, these ants, these insects, these fish, these birds, this nightingale, these reptiles, these animals, this never-ending beauty and delight of the eye.

﴿فَسُبْحَـٰنَ ٱللَّهِ حِينَ تُمْسُونَ وَحِينَ تُصْبِحُونَ ۝ وَلَهُ ٱلْحَمْدُ فِى ٱلسَّمَـٰوَٰتِ وَٱلْأَرْضِ وَعَشِيًّا وَحِينَ تُظْهِرُونَ ۝ يُخْرِجُ ٱلْحَىَّ مِنَ ٱلْمَيِّتِ وَيُخْرِجُ ٱلْمَيِّتَ مِنَ ٱلْحَىِّ وَيُحْىِ ٱلْأَرْضَ بَعْدَ مَوْتِهَا وَكَذَٰلِكَ تُخْرَجُونَ ۝﴾

(سورة الرُّوم: ١٧-١٩)

❨So exalted is Allah when you reach the evening and when you reach the morning. And to Him is [due all] praise throughout the heavens and the earth. And [exalted is He] at night and when you are at noon. He brings the living out of the dead and brings the dead out of the living and brings to life the earth after its lifelessness. And thus will you be brought out.❩

(Qur'an 30: 17-19)

"Do not look at the negative aspects of life; be content with the beauty and joy of it."

❨And stay in your houses...❩

(Qur'an 33: 33)

10
The ultimate honour and infinite generosity

The Byzantines captured some of the Muslim women, and al-Manṣūr ibn 'Ammār heard the news. They said to him: "Why don't you go and sit near the caliph and urge the people to attack?" So he went and sat near the caliph, Harūn ar-Rashīd, in ar-Raqqah, near Damascus.

Whilst shaykh Manṣūr was urging people to fight in *jihād* (fighting for the sake of Allah), a tied-up bundle with a letter attached was thrown to him. Manṣūr opened the letter and in it he read: "I am a woman from among the Arab clans. I heard what the Byzantines did to the Muslim women, and I heard that you are urging the people to attack. I looked for the most honourable thing on my body, and it was my two braids, so I cut them off and wrapped them in this bundle. I urge you by Almighty Allah to make them into a bridle for the horse of a warrior fighting for the sake of Allah. Perhaps Allah will look upon me and have mercy on me because of them."

Manṣūr could not control his feelings when he read these noble words. He wept and made the people weep with him. Then Harūn ar-Rashīd launched a general mobilization, and he himself fought alongside the *mujāhidīn* (fighters for the sake of Allah), and Allah, the Exalted, granted them victory.

"Do not weep for the past and do not

shed tears for no reason, for you
cannot bring back the past."

Chapter 8

Chapter 8

❨... Verily, in the remembrance of Allah
do hearts find rest.❩ *(Qur'an 13: 28)*

1
You have nowhere to turn but to Allah

A man entered the mosque when it was not the time for prayer, and he found a ten-year-old boy praying with proper focus and humility. He waited until the boy had finished praying, then he came, greeted him and said: "Whose son are you?" The boy lowered his head and a tear rolled down his cheek, then he raised his head and said: "O' uncle, I am an orphan who has no father or mother." The man felt sorry for him and said: "Would you like to be my son?"

The boy said: "If I get hungry will you feed me?"

"Yes."

"If I am naked will you clothe me?"

"Yes."

"If I fall sick will you heal me?"

"I am not able to do that, my son."

"If I die will you bring me back to life?"

"I am not able to do that."

The boy said, "Then leave me, my uncle, to the One Who created me, for He will guide me and He is the one who gives me food and drink. If I fall sick He heals me and He is the One Who, I hope, will forgive me on the Day of Judgement."

The man fell silent and went on his way, saying, "I believe in Allah, whoever puts his trust in Allah, Allah will suffice him."

> "No matter how much you pull your hair, or allow your throat to be overwhelmed by grief and despair, you will not be able to bring back any one of past events."

❨... And My Mercy embraces all things...❩

(Qur'an 7: 156)

2
Happiness exists...
but who can find it?

No person can find happiness except in himself, but he has to be guided to the best way of finding it, which may be summed up as the need to be sincere, courageous, hard-working, loving towards people, cooperative and unselfish. And he should have a conscience above all else. Happiness is not a myth, it is something very real, and is enjoyed by many. We can enjoy it too, if we learn from experience and benefit from what we have gone through in life. If we are patient, we can explore and learn much from ourselves; we can rid ourselves of many physical and psychological diseases with knowledge, will-power and patience, and we can live the lives that Allah has given us, without ingratitude, disobedience or misery.

"There is nothing more damaging to a woman's beauty than anxiety that makes her look older than her age."

{And verily, your Lord will give you [all good]
so that you shall be well-pleased.} *(Qur'an 93: 5)*

3
A good attitude is a great blessing

People are the mirror of the individual. If he behaves well towards them they will behave well towards him, so his nerves will be calmed, and he will be content, and he will feel that he is living in a friendly environment.

But if a person treats others badly and is harsh towards them, he will find that people treat him badly and in a rough and harsh manner. Whoever does not respect people will not be respected by them.

The one who has a good attitude will have more peace of mind and is less likely to be anxious and distressed or find himself in painful situations. In addition to that, having a good attitude is an act of worship to Allah, the Exalted, and is something that He encourages a great deal.

Allah, the Exalted, says:

﴿خُذِ ٱلْعَفْوَ وَأْمُرْ بِٱلْعُرْفِ وَأَعْرِضْ عَنِ ٱلْجَٰهِلِينَ ۝﴾

(سورة الأعراف : ١٩٩)

{Show forgiveness, enjoin what is good, and turn away from the ignorant.} *(Qur'an 7: 199)*

﴿فَبِمَا رَحْمَةٍ مِّنَ ٱللَّهِ لِنتَ لَهُمْ وَلَوْ كُنتَ فَظًّا غَلِيظَ ٱلْقَلْبِ لَٱنفَضُّوا۟ مِنْ حَوْلِكَ فَٱعْفُ عَنْهُمْ وَٱسْتَغْفِرْ لَهُمْ وَشَاوِرْهُمْ فِى﴾

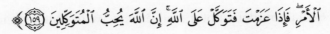

(سورة آل عِمرَان: ١٥٩)

❨And by the Mercy of Allah, you dealt with them gently. And had you been severe and harsh-hearted, they would have broken away from about you; so pass over [their faults], and ask [Allah's] forgiveness for them; and consult them in the affairs. Then when you have taken a decision, rely upon Allah, certainly, Allah loves those who rely [upon Him].❩

(Qur'an 3: 159)

The Messenger of Allah (Blessings and Peace be upon him) said: *"The most beloved of you to me are those who are best in attitude and humble, who get along with people and people get along with them. The most disliked of you to me are those who walk around spreading malicious gossip and causing division between friends, those who seek out the faults of the innocent."*

"Hesitation, languor and going around a problem without hope, all lead to nervous breakdown."

❰Allah burdens not a soul except [with that within]
its capacity...❱ *(Qur'an 2: 286)*

4
How to achieve a happy life

An American psychologist said: Living a happy life is a fine art which entails ten things:

1.   Do a work that you love. If you cannot do that, then find a hobby that you love and do it in your spare time and reinforce it.

2.   Take care of your health for it is the spirit of happiness. This means being moderate in eating and drinking, exercising regularly and avoiding bad habits.

3.   Have a goal in life, for this will give you motivation and energy.

4.   Take life as it comes, and accept the bitter and the sweet.

5.   Live in the present, with no regret for the past and no anxiety about tomorrow that has not come yet.

6.   Think hard about any action or decision, and do not blame anyone else for your decision or its consequences.

7.   Look at those who are worse off than you.

8.   Have the habit of smiling and being cheerful, and keep company with optimistic people.

9.   Strive to make others happy so that you may benefit from the atmosphere of happiness.

10. Make the most of occasions of happiness and joy, and regard them as necessary to renew your own happiness.

> "Enjoy today and make the most of it; look for things that will prevent pain from happening before it attacks you."

❬Every day He is [engaged] in some affair [such as giving honour or disgrace to some, life or death to some]!❭

(Qur'an 55: 29)

5
Seek refuge with Allah from worry and grief

I do not think that a wise man would do away with smiling or that a believer would be inclined to be pessimistic and filled with despair. A person may be exposed to circumstances that take away his peace of mind and tranquility, but, in that case, he has to trust that Allah, the Almighty, will save him from what has befallen him. If he gives in to depression, that will mark the beginning of a total collapse of his will, and all his deeds will be affected by helplessness and incapacity.

Hence, the Messenger of Allah (Blessings and Peace be upon him) used to teach his Companions to seek the help of Allah to solve their problems. Abu Sa'īd al-Khudri said: *"The Messenger of Allah entered the mosque one day, and saw a man from among the Anṣār, whose name was Abu Umāmah. He said: 'O' Abu Umāmah, why do I see you sitting in the mosque when it is not the time for prayer?' He said: 'Worries and debts, O' Messenger of Allah.' He said: 'Shall I not teach you some words which, if you say them, Allah will take away your worries and pay off your debts?' He said, 'Yes, O' Messenger of Allah.' He said: 'Say, in the morning and the evening*:

Allahumma inni a'ūdhu bika min al-hamm wa al-ḥuzan, wa a'ūdhu bika min al-'ajzi wal-kasal, wa a'ūdhu bika min al-bukhli wal-jubn, wa a'ūdhu bika min ghalbat ad-dayn wa qahr ar-rijāli (O' Allah, I seek refuge with You from distress and grief, and I seek refuge with You from incapacity and laziness, and I seek refuge with You from miserliness and cowardice, and I seek refuge with You from the burden of debt and from being overpowered by men).'" (Narrated by Abu Dāwūd)

He (Abu Umāmah) said: "I did that, and Allah took away my worries and paid off my debt for me."

> "An ulcer is not the result of what you consume, it is the result of what consumes you."

⁕And whatever of blessings [and good things]
you have, it is from Allah...⁕ *(Qur'an 16: 53)*

6
The woman who offers support at the time of calamity

In *at-Tabaqāt*, it is narrated that Fāṭimah az-Zahrā' (may Allah be pleased with her), the daughter of the Messenger of Allah (Blessings and Peace be upon him), used to go hungry for days. One day her husband 'Ali (may Allah be pleased with him) noticed that she looked pale, and asked her, "What is the matter with you, O' Fāṭimah?" She said, "For three days we have not found anything to eat in the house." He said: "Why did you not tell me?" She said: "My father, the Messenger of Allah, told me on the night I got married: 'O' Fāṭimah, if 'Ali brings you something then eat it, and if he does not, then do not ask him.'"

But many women specialize in emptying their husbands' pockets. As soon as they see some money there, they declare a state of emergency in the house, and do not calm down until they have taken everything.

Undoubtedly, if a man gives in once, this problem will never end and disputes will eventually arise, which may ultimately result in divorce.

"Life is too short to shorten it further,
so do not try to make it shorter."

"Success means that your name is on everyone's lips."

7

A woman from among the people of Paradise

'Aṭā' ibn Abi Rabāḥ narrated: Ibn 'Abbās (may Allah be pleased with him) said to me: "Shall I not show you a woman from among the people of Paradise?" I said, "Yes." He said: "This black woman came to the Prophet (Blessings and Peace be upon him) and said: 'I suffer from epilepsy, and I become uncovered. Pray to Allah for me.' He said: 'If you wish, you can bear it with patience and Paradise will be yours, or if you wish I can pray to Allah to heal you.' She said: 'I will be patient, but I become uncovered; pray to Allah that I will not become uncovered.' So he prayed for her."

This pious, believing woman accepted a problem that stayed with her throughout her transient worldly life, so that she could attain Paradise. She made a good deal, for she was one of the people of Paradise. But she did not like to become uncovered so that people could see her *'awrah* (all body except hand and face), which is not befitting for a pious, modest, Muslim woman. So, what should we say to those women who are clothed yet naked, who try hard to show off their charms and to cast aside the veil of modesty and appear virtually naked?

"Enough of anxiety! Be patient and face reality with steadfastness; fill your time and keep going."

"Help comes according to ability (provision)."

8
Charity wards off calamity

Charity is an important means of finding peace of mind. If a person does good deeds, Allah rewards him in this world by granting him a sense of tranquility and contentment. So, give in charity even if it is a little, and do not think of anything that you give as insignificant, even if it is just one date, or one mouthful of food, or a sip of water or milk. Give to the poor and destitute, feed the hungry, and visit the sick. Then you will find that Allah will reduce your worries and grief. Charity is a remedy which can only be found in the pharmacy of Islam.

A man asked Imam 'Abdullāh ibn al-Mubārak: "O' Abu 'Abd ar-Raḥmān, I have had an abscess on my knee for seven years. I asked doctors about it and tried all kinds of remedies, but nothing worked."

Ibn al-Mubārak said to him: "Go and look for a place where people are in need of water, and dig a well there, and I hope that when the water bubbles forth the bleeding from your knee will stop." The man did that and was cured.

This comes as no surprise, for the Messenger of Allah (Blessings and Peace be upon him) said: *"Treat your sick ones with charity,"* and he also said: *"Charity extinguishes the wrath of the Lord and wards off a bad end."*

"Anxiety is the friend of idleness."

❨*Ḥoor* [beautiful, fair females] guarded in pavilions...❩
(Qur'an 55: 72)

9

Be beautiful in spirit because the universe is beautiful

The stars in the sky are so beautiful, there is no doubt about it. Their beauty takes the breath away. It varies according to the time of day; it is different from morning to evening, from sunrise to sunset, from a moonlit night to a dark night, from a clear sky to a foggy and cloudy sky. It may even differ from one moment to another, from one observation point to another, from one angle to another. But all of it is beautiful and breathtaking.

This one star that is twinkling here is like a beautiful eye shining with love. These two stars standing alone have slipped away from the crowd to converse intimately with each other. This constellation of stars grouped together like a circle of friends chatting at a party in heaven. This dreaming moon, wandering from night to night, sometimes shining brightly and sometimes dimmed, sometimes like a newborn and sometimes slipping away as if to oblivion.

This vast space, which the eye can never tire of looking at its vastness, eyesight can never reach its ends.

It is all beautiful, and man can only look at it and ponder, but he cannot describe it with the words that he possesses.

"You should accept the inevitable, but if you worry about it, how will that help?"

❨... And do not display yourselves like that
of the times of ignorance...❩

(Qur'an 33: 33)

10
A hero Woman

The caliph 'Uthmān ibn 'Affān (may Allah be pleased with him) appointed Ḥabīb ibn Maslamah al-Fihri to lead a Muslim army against the Byzantines, who had provoked the Muslims. The wife of Ḥabīb was also a soldier in this army. Before the battle began, Ḥabīb started checking on his army, and his wife came and asked him: "Where will we meet when the fighting becomes intense and the ranks of the army are moving like waves?"

He replied: "You will find me either in the tent of the Byzantine commander, or in Paradise." The fighting grew intense and Ḥabīb and his companions fought bravely as never before. Allah granted them victory over the Byzantines, and Ḥabīb rushed to the tent of the Byzantine commander to wait for his wife. When he reached the door of the tent, he found something amazing: his wife had got there before him and already entered the tent of the Byzantine commander.

"There is nothing difficult or impossible in life so long as you are able to work and move."

Chapter 9

❨Therefore, remember Me [by praying, glorifying].
I will remember you...❩

(Qur'an 2: 152)

1
Do not spend your time doing nothing

Your Prophet (Blessings and Peace be upon him) said to 'Ā'ishah (may Allah be pleased with her): *"If you commit a sin, then ask Allah for forgiveness and repent to Him, for if a person acknowledges his sin and repents, Allah will accept his repentance."*

Imagine that you possess all the money you ever wanted and achieved all your dreams and fulfilled all your wishes, then you lost everything. You would weep and complain, and be filled with regret; you would bite your fingers in sorrow for what you have lost. So what about your life which is slipping away from you without you even realizing it?

Your life is a precious jewel whose value cannot be measured in material terms. Every minute of your life that passes can never come back. These minutes are your capital in this world, with which you can buy whatever you want of the delights of Paradise. How can you waste this life without repenting sincerely?

"There is one way that leads to happiness: stop being worried about the things beyond your control."

❨... So Allah will suffice for you against them...❩

(Qur'an 2: 137)

2
Happiness cannot be bought with money

There are men who spend their youth and health to accumulate wealth, then they spend the rest of their lives spending all that they have acquired in an attempt to buy happiness, but all they get is misery. Or they try to reclaim their youth, but old age overtakes them. Or they try to get their health back, but incurable disease overtakes them.

A famous actor said that all he ever wanted in life was money.

He thought that with money he would be able to be the happiest man in the world for a hundred years! He was confident that if he had money he would be able to achieve all he wished and that everything he hoped for would fall into his hands. After twenty years, Allah gave him more money than he had wished for, but He took away his health and his youth and dreams! It was reported that he used to cry and say: "I wish I had never asked Allah for money; I wish that I had asked Him to let me live for a hundred years in poverty, eating *cooked broad beans*, jumping on the steps of the streetcar to avoid paying the fare." This actor never knew the values of good health until he lost it, and he never realized that money cannot buy everything, until he became the most famous actor in Egypt, and he realized that he could not add a single day to his life that was drawing to an end.

"You should not spend half your life
in disputes."

❨And seek help through patience and

aṣ-Ṣalāh [the prayer]...❩

(Qur'an 2: 45)

3

Haste and recklessness are the fuel of misery

Patience is like a knight that can defeat foolish desires. Deliberation means being certain and not being hasty, and taking action based on rational thought and wisdom. These two characteristics can defeat anxiety; whoever is lacking in them is missing out on a lot of goodness and will suffer a great deal of anxiety. The patient person can ward off many evils, but the fool does not control his anger and lets evil increase and the causes of anxiety grow greater and take root. The person who is deliberate seldom feels regret or does something whose consequences are unknown. But the foolish and hasty person is no stranger to regret, anxiety and bad consequences. Similarly, if a person is kind to himself and others, he will be successful and will be used to being calm and will have peace of mind.

Our religion of Islam encourages us to be kind, patient and forbearing. The Messenger of Allah (Blessings and Peace be upon him) said: *"There is never any kindness in a thing but it makes it beautiful, and it is never lacking in a thing without making it ugly."*

"We waste our happy times for valueless things."

❨... And [Allah] has not laid upon you in religion
any hardship...❩ *(Qur'an 22: 78)*

4
The game of accumulating wealth has no end

Beaverbrook said: "I accumulated a great deal of wealth, but I realized from experience that persisting in that game — the game of accumulating wealth — was very dangerous and had no end, and it would consume my life and happiness. So, I changed my profession and found a job I liked in the publishing field, which did not generate much wealth, but it brought me happiness and served society. I advise every man who has accumulated enough wealth to suffice him, to stop playing this money-game and retire early, so he can enjoy what he has achieved and plan to do work that he likes, so that he can serve society and enjoy his time."

The one who has an accumulated wealth has little concern about leaving behind a large estate for his heirs, because he knows that they will be better men if they go out into the world having little wealth and with nothing but their brains and attitudes. Wealth without effort often becomes a curse rather than a blessing, misery rather than happiness. When men are able to satisfy their physical desires in luxury and laziness, their minds become occupied with petty and idle pursuits, and their youth fades away until they die.

"Have strong faith that nothing is impossible in life."

❰... O' fire! Be coolness and safety upon Ibrāhīm [Abraham].❱

(Qur'an 21: 69)

5

Immorality is generated by idleness

In the lap of idleness, immorality is born and the germs of death and oblivion are generated. But if the mission of the living is to be active, then the idle are dead.

If this world is a preparation for a greater life that is to come hereafter, then the idle deserve to be gathered penniless, with no harvest but loss and doom.

The Prophet (Blessings and Peace be upon him) pointed out that there are thousands who are unaware of the blessings of wealth and free time that have been bestowed upon them. He said: *"There are two blessings of which many people are careless: good health and free time."*

How many sound-bodied people go about in life with no goal to drive them, nothing to occupy them, no mission to devote their life to and try their best to make it succeed?

Is this what man was created for? Not at all. Allah, says:

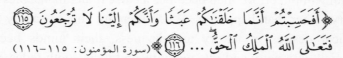

❰Did you think that We had created you in play [without any purpose], and that you would not be brought back to Us? So Exalted is Allah, the Sovereign, the Truth...❱   *(Qur'an 23: 115-116)*

Life was created for a purpose, so were the heavens, the earth and everything in between. Man should understand the purpose (behind this creation) and live for it.

But if he dwells in the shadow of his narrow desires and hides away blinkered by their limitations, then what a bad choice that is for his present and his future.

> "Always bear in mind the picture
> of success and keep it alive in
> your mind."

❨And He will provide him from [sources]
he never could imagine...❩

(Qur'an 65: 3)

6
A house without anger, noise
and exhaustion

She said to her father, weeping: "O' my father, there was a problem between me and my husband yesterday, because of something I said. When I saw how angry he was I regretted what I had done, and I apologized to him, but he refused to speak to me and turned his face away from me. I kept on trying to calm him down until he smiled and was pleased with me. I am afraid that my Lord will hold me accountable for those moments in which I drove him crazy, when he was angry." Her father said to her: "O' my daughter, by the One in Whose hand is my soul, if you had died before your husband was pleased with you, Allah would not have been pleased with you. Don't you know that the woman whose husband is angry with her is cursed in the *Tawrāt* (Torah), the *Injīl* (Gospel) and the Qur'an, and the throes of death will be difficult for her, and her grave will be made narrow for her? So, glad tidings to the woman whose husband is pleased with her."

The righteous woman is keen to be dear to her husband, so she does not do anything to upset their life together.

"Dismiss the idea of failure out of your mind."

"There is no peace of mind for the one who has no faith."

7

Chastity and modesty enhance beauty

Have you heard the story of Umm Salamah (may Allah be pleased with her), the wife of the Prophet (Blessings and Peace be upon him), when she heard him say, *"Whoever drags his garment out of pride, Allah will not look at him on the Day of Resurrection?"* She said: *"What should women do with their hems?"* He said, *"Lengthen them by a handspan."* She said: *"But then their feet will show."* He said: *"Lengthen them by a cubit, but no more than that."*

What a good example Umm Salamah was. She was not one of those who show off and are arrogant. Muslim women should be modest and chaste, pure and noble. Their feet should not show and their clothes should have long hemlines that drag along the ground behind them so that men will not see anything of them. But women nowadays — except for those on whom Allah has mercy — raise their hemlines as much as they can, for fear of getting them wet or dirty, and in imitation of the disbelieving women who appear virtually naked. They make a thousand excuses for appearing as if naked and for behaving in an immoral manner — there is no strength and no power except with Allah. Their menfolk are men only in name, walking at their side and not caring about the loss of modesty.

"Physical well-being comes from
eating little, mental well-being comes

from sinning little, well-being of the heart comes from worrying little and well-being of the tongue comes from speaking little."

"The patient person gets the best results."

8
Allah may bring the absent person back home

After a long separation of more than twenty years, Allah decreed that a woman and her twenty-five-year old daughter should be reunited, after being separated by circumstances. This happened when the daughter was spending her honeymoon in the Jibāl (mountains) as-Sawdah resort in Abha.

The mother had remarried after her first husband left her, when her daughter was three years old. Her new husband's circumstances and continual moves from one city to another prevented her from seeing her daughter, whom she had left in the care of her father.

One beautiful summer day in Jibāl as-Sawdah in Abha, the daughter met a lady in the resort. They started chatting, and neither of them knew the other. The mother had left her daughter when she was three years old. Whilst they were chatting, the mother noticed that one of the girl's fingers was missing, and she asked her about her mother. The girl told her her story, and the mother realized that she was face to face with the daughter whom she had lost twenty years ago. She took her in her arms and kissed her face, filled with compassion and love, and told her how much she had missed her for all those years.

"Thinking of happiness will inevitably

lead to thinking of what comes before
and after, and that, in itself, spoils
the sense of happiness."

⦗As if they were rubies and coral...⦘

(Qur'an 55: 58)

9
One phrase may fill time and space

Mūsa (may Allah's peace be upon him) said: "O' Lord, teach me a *du'ā'* with which I may call upon You and converse with You." He said: "O' Mūsa, say: *Lā ilāha illallah* (there is no god but Allah)." Mūsa said: "All the people say, *Lā ilāha illallah.*" He said: "O' Mūsa, if the seven heavens and the earth were to be placed in one side (of the balance) and *Lā ilāha illallah* in the other, *Lā ilāha illallah* would outweigh them."

Lā ilāha illallah... are brilliant words which disperse the fog of sin. They bring light, but those who say these words vary in the degree of light, how strong or weak it is, no one knows except Allah, the Exalted.

For some people, the light of these words in their hearts is like the sun; for others it is like a bright star; for others it is like a mighty torch, or a bright lamp, or a feebly flickering lamp.

The greater the light of these words is, the more efficiently it burns away doubts, whims and desires.

"The happiness of the believer lies in loving Allah, and love for the sake of Allah brings deeper happiness whose taste is known to sincere believers who do not accept any substitute for it."

"Woman is more precious than treasure and wealth."

10
Hearts longing for Paradise

Have you heard the story of a righteous woman, whose husband died, leaving her with two children? When they grew up, the first thing she taught them was to worship and obey Allah, and to pray *qiyām al-layl* (night prayers).

She said to her sons: "No moment of the night should pass in our house without someone standing in prayer and remembering Allah." They said: "What do you mean, O' Mother?" She said: "We will divide the night in three. One of you should stand and pray for the first third, and the other for the second third, then I will stand and pray for the last third, and then wake you up to pray *Fajr* (dawn)."

They said: "We hear and obey, O' Mother." When the mother died, the two sons did not give up praying *qiyām al-layl*, because their hearts were filled with the love of obedience and worship, and the sweetest moments of their lives were when they stood and prayed at night. So they divided the night between them. When one of them became very sick, the other stood and prayed for the whole night.

"Life around us with all its beauty and nobility is a real invitation to happiness."

Chapter 10

❨... And if you count the favour [Blessings] of Allah, you
could not enumerate them...❩

(Qur'an 14: 34)

1
Belief in the divine will and decree, both good and bad

Allah, the Almighty, All-Glorious, says:

﴿وَمَآ أَصَابَ مِن مُّصِيبَةٍ فِي ٱلْأَرْضِ وَلَا فِيٓ أَنفُسِكُمْ إِلَّا فِي
كِتَٰبٍ مِّن قَبْلِ أَن نَّبْرَأَهَآ إِنَّ ذَٰلِكَ عَلَى ٱللَّهِ يَسِيرٌ ۝
لِّكَيْلَا تَأْسَوْاْ عَلَىٰ مَا فَاتَكُمْ وَلَا تَفْرَحُواْ بِمَآ ءَاتَىٰكُمْ وَٱللَّهُ لَا
يُحِبُّ كُلَّ مُخْتَالٍ فَخُورٍ ۝﴾ (سورة الحَديد: ٢٢-٢٣)

❨No calamity befalls on the earth or in yourselves but
it is inscribed in the Book of Decrees (*al-Lawḥ al-
Maḥfūẓ*) before We bring it into existence. Verily, that
is easy for Allah. In order that you may not grieve at
the things over that you fail to get, nor rejoice over
what He has given to you. And Allah likes not
prideful boasters.❩ *(Qur'an 57: 22-23)*

﴿ ... وَعَسَىٰٓ أَن تَكْرَهُواْ شَيْئًا وَهُوَ خَيْرٌ لَّكُمْ وَعَسَىٰٓ أَن
تُحِبُّواْ شَيْئًا وَهُوَ شَرٌّ لَّكُمْ وَٱللَّهُ يَعْلَمُ وَأَنتُمْ لَا تَعْلَمُونَ
﴾ (سورة البَقَرَة: ٢١٦)

❨... And it may be that you dislike a thing which is
good for you and that you like a thing which is bad

for you. Allah knows but you do not know.⟩

(Qur'an 2: 216)

Belief in the divine will and decree plays a major role in bringing peace of mind at times of calamity, especially when a person understands fully that Allah is kind to His slaves and wants things to be easy for them, and He is wise and saves (reward) for them in the Hereafter, so that He will give the patient their reward in abundance. If we think and act upon this, it will turn the grief and distress of calamity into happiness and joy, but not everyone is able to do that.

What are the steps that we may take to reduce depression and lessen the impact of calamity?

1.   Imagine that the calamity could be greater than what it is, with worse consequences.

2.   Think about those who are faced with a greater calamity.

3.   Look at the blessings that you do have, of which many are deprived.

4.   Do not give in to the feelings of frustration which may come along with calamity:

$$\text{﴿فَإِنَّ مَعَ ٱلْعُسْرِ يُسْرًا ۝ إِنَّ مَعَ ٱلْعُسْرِ يُسْرًا ۝﴾}$$

(سورة الشَّرح: ٥–٦)

⟨Verily, along with every hardship is relief, Verily, along with every hardship is relief.⟩

(Qur'an 94: 5-6)

> "Of quickest messages of happiness to others is a sincere smile from the heart."

{None besides Allah can avert it [or advance it
or delay it — the Day of Resurrection].}

(Qur'an 53: 58)

2
The best things are those that are moderate

Muṣṭafa Maḥmoud said:

"I feel happy because I am an average man with an average income. My health is average, my standard of living is average and I have a little of everything, which means that I have a lot of motivation, and motivation is life. The motivation in our hearts is the true warmth of life, the basis on which we evaluate our happiness.

I pray to Allah that He may bless the reader of these lines with an average life, and give him a little of everything... this is a good prayer, I swear by Allah the Almighty.

My mother did not know much about philosophy, but she had common sense and she understood what I am saying without having read about it. She used to call that contentment, and contentment means having enough, having a little of everything and a great deal of spiritual energy."

"A false smile is a blunt sign of hypocrisy."

"My delight of the eye is in prayer."   (Hadith)

3
The pessimist creates
an atmosphere of depression

A person influences the mood and attitude of his companion. If a person — be it a friend, a life-partner or a colleague — is calm, cheerful and optimistic, then he will transmit these good characteristics to his companion.

But if he is frowning and miserable, fed up with life, always worried and pessimistic, then he will transfer this bleak anxiety to his companion like a contagious disease.

It is not just people who can have this effect. There are books, TV shows and radio programmes as well. Some are optimistic and some are pessimistic; some provoke anxiety and some promote peace of mind. Books, especially, are like seasons, some are like spring and some are like autumn. If a person is guided to choose optimistic books that celebrate life and encourage one to strive, succeed and be confident, then he will have done himself a favour. But if he chooses books that cause worry and provoke doubts about values and human nature, and that are pessimistic about life and mankind, then he will be influenced by their contagion as a leper affects a healthy man, and that may disrupt his life.

"The way to happiness is in front of you, so seek it by means of knowledge, righteous deeds and a good attitude. Be moderate in all your affairs and you will be happy."

❨*... And He sent down as-Sakīnah* [calmness and tranquillity] *upon them...*❩ *(Qur'an 48: 18)*

4
Beware of complaining and being discontent

An old and wise man said:

"When I was in my twenties and thirties, I used to moan and complain even when I was enjoying myself, because I did not know that I was happy. Now that I am over sixty, I know fully well how happy I was when I was in my twenties and thirties. But that knowledge came too late. I have no more than memories, and memories are regrets. If I had understood on time, I would have lived with great joy. I would not have found any reason to complain when I was in the primrose of my youth, which I can only see now that it and I are fading."

To you, dear reader, I say:

Either you will be aware of your happiness and enjoy it with all your senses, or you will ignore that and look elsewhere for what you think you are lacking, in which case you will fall prey to complaining and discontent. In that case, wait until this present becomes the past, then you will weep and realize how happy you were at that time, but you did not realize it, but now you have nothing left but fading memories.

"A woman may turn the home into a paradise or into an unbearable hell."

❴... Allah being pleased with them and they with Him...❵

(Qur'an 5: 119)

5
Most problems have petty causes

Unfortunately, trivial matters often cause thousands of people to lose their common sense; families are broken up and friendships destroyed, and people are left confused and broken. Dale Carnegie explains the consequences of being provoked by petty things: "Petty things in a marriage could drive both partners mad and they are the cause of half of the heartache suffered in this world."

This is what is confirmed by the experts. After ruling in more than forty thousand cases of divorce, Joseph Sabath, a Chicago judge, said: "You will always find that trivial matters are behind the failure of a marriage."

Frank Hogan, the public prosecutor in New York, stated that half of the cases brought to the criminal court are the result of petty causes, such as an argument between family members, an unintended slight, a hurtful word or an offensive gesture. These insignificant things lead to killing and other crimes.

Very few of us are wicked and hard-hearted by nature, but ongoing blows directed at our pride and dignity are the cause of half the problems in the world.

"The greatest blessing is goodness in the soul which makes one happy."

❴[Remember] when you sought help of your Lord
and He answered you...❵

(Qur'an 8: 9)

6
Restraining the tongue

The historians narrate that one day Khālid ibn Yazīd ibn Mu'āwiyah slandered 'Abdullāh ibn az-Zubayr, the sworn enemy of Bani Umayyah, and said that he was a miser. His wife Ramlah bint az-Zubayr, the sister of 'Abdullāh, was sitting there, but she kept quiet and did not say a word. Khālid said to her: "Why don't you say anything? Do you agree with what I said, or is it just that you do not want to answer me?" She said: "Neither. But a woman was not created to interfere in the affairs of men, rather, we are flowers for smelling and embracing. Why would we want to interfere in your affairs?" He was impressed with her words and kissed her between the eyes.

The Messenger of Allah (Blessings and Peace be upon him) emphatically forbade spreading the secrets of the marital relationship. Aḥmad ibn Ḥanbal narrated that Asmā' bint Yazīd said that she was with the Prophet (Blessings and Peace be upon him) and men and women were sitting there, and he said: *"Perhaps a man says what he does with his wife, or perhaps a woman says what she does with her husband."* The people kept quiet and did not respond. I said: "O' Messenger of Allah, they do indeed do that." He said: "Do not do that, for that is as if a male devil met a female devil in the street and had intercourse with her whilst the people were looking on."*

Some *mufassirīn* (commentators) interpret the word *ḥāfiẓāt* [(women) who guard] in the verse,

﴿ ... فَٱلصَّٰلِحَٰتُ قَٰنِتَٰتٌ حَٰفِظَٰتٌ لِّلْغَيْبِ بِمَا حَفِظَ ٱللَّهُ ... ﴿٣٤﴾ ﴾

(سورة النِّسَاء: ٣٤)

❨... Therefore the righteous women are devoutly obedient [to Allah and to their husbands], and guard in [the husband's] absence what Allah orders them to guard...❩
(Qur'an 4: 34)

— as referring to women who guard (keep secret) what happens between them and their husbands.

"Count Allah's blessings upon you,
not your problems."

"Life is short; don't make it even shorter by worrying."

7
Fight anxiety by praying

The first Muslim women knew that prayer was the link between a person and his or her Lord, and that those who pray with proper focus and humility are the ones who are successful.

(سورة المؤمنون: ١-٢)

❮Successful indeed are the believers. Those who offer their *Ṣalāh* [prayers] with all solemnity and full submissiveness.❯   *(Qur'an 23: 1-2)*

They used to stay up at night, worshipping with full humility and submission. They knew that the best provision for the Hereafter, and the thing that helps make the message reach the people, is prayer. It gives a person will-power and helps to resolve difficulties and face hardship. They also knew that praying *qiyām al-layl* is one of the best acts of worship that bring a person closer to Allah, the Exalted, as He said to the first *dā'iyah* [the Prophet (Blessings and Peace be upon him)]:

﴿وَمِنَ ٱلَّيۡلِ فَتَهَجَّدۡ بِهِۦ نَافِلَةٗ لَّكَ عَسَىٰٓ أَن يَبۡعَثَكَ رَبُّكَ مَقَامٗا مَّحۡمُودٗا ٧٩﴾

(سورة الإسراء: ٧٩)

❮And in some parts of the night [also] offer the *Ṣalāh* [prayer] with it [i.e. recite the Qur'an in the prayer] as an additional prayer [*Tahajjud* (spending the night in prayers)] and optional prayer [*Nawāfil*] for you [O'

Muhammad]. It may be that your Lord will raise you
to *Maqām Maḥmūd* [a station of praise and glory, i.e.,
the honour of intercession on the Day of Resurrec-
tion].❩
                                          (Qur'an 17: 79)

And He praises those who pray *qiyām al-layl*:

﴿كَانُوا۟ قَلِيلًا مِّنَ ٱلَّيْلِ مَا يَهْجَعُونَ ۝﴾   (سورة الذاريات : ١٧)

❨They used to sleep but little of the night [invoking
their Lord (Allah) and praying, with fear and hope]
...❩
                                          (Qur'an 51: 17)

Anas (may Allah be pleased with him) narrated that, "*The
Prophet (Blessings and Peace be upon him) entered the mosque
and saw a rope tied between two of the pillars of the mosque. He
said: 'What is this rope?' They said: 'It belongs to Zaynab. When
she feels tired she holds on to it.' The Prophet said: 'Untie it. Let
any one of you pray when he has the energy, and when he feels
tired, let him sit down.'*" The believing women used to force
themselves to pray at night, seeking the pleasure of Allah, but the
Prophet (Blessings and Peace be upon him) commanded them not
to impose on themselves more than they could bear. The best of
worship is that which is done regularly, even if it is a little. We
know that the women of the modern age fill their time, night and
day, with worldly things, but the least that is expected of them is
two *rak'ahs* offered in the middle of the night to defeat the
Shayṭān (Satan) thereby. The best of matters are those that are
moderate, and "those who go to extremes are doomed" as the
Messenger of Allah (Blessings and Peace be upon him) said.

> "Put your trust in Allah if you are
> sincere, and rejoice in tomorrow if
> you are repentant."

"Patience is the key to relief."

8
Advice of a successful woman

A modern mother offered her daughter the following advice, accompanied with smiles and tears:

O' my daughter, you are about to embark on a new life — a life in which there is no room for your father and mother, or for any of your brothers and sisters. In this new life, you will become a companion to your husband who will not want to share you with anyone, not even your own flesh and blood.

Be a wife to him and a mother. Make him feel that you are everything to him in this life. Always remember that a man, any man, is a big child and any sweet word will make him happy. Do not make him feel that by marrying you he has deprived you of your own family, for he is experiencing similar feelings himself. He has also left his parents' house and left his family for your sake. But the difference between him and you is the difference between man and woman; a woman always longs for her family and the house in which she was born and grew up. But she has to resign herself to this new life and adapt to living with this man who has become her husband and who will be the father of her children... this is your new world.

My daughter! this is your present and your future, this is your family which you and your husband will make together. I am not asking you to forget your father and mother and siblings, because they will never forget you. How can a mother forget the child who is the apple of her eye? But I am asking you to love your husband and live with him and be happy in your life with him.

"Learn patience from Āsiyah, loyalty from Khadījah, sincerity from 'Ā'ishah and steadfastness from Fāṭimah."

❨Whom no man or jinni has touched before them...❩

(Qur'an 55: 74)

9

Whoever does not find comfort in Allah will not find comfort in anything else

Allah, the Almighty, is the source of comfort and joy for the believers and those who obey Him, and the most beloved to those who worship Him. Whoever finds comfort in Him will be happy and will enjoy life. His heart will be at peace and filled with life and love of Allah; Whose Attributes will live in his conscience and he will always bear the names of Allah in mind. He will remember Allah's names and ponder over His Attributes; his mind will be filled with thoughts of *ar-Raḥmān* (the Most Gracious), *ar-Raḥīm* (the Most Merciful), *al-Ḥamīd* (the Praiseworthy), *al-Ḥalīm* (the Forbearing), *al-Barr* (the Source of Goodness), *al-Laṭīf* (the Most Subtle and Courteous), *al-Muḥsin* (the Beneficent), *al-Wadūd* (the Loving), *al-Karīm* (the Most Generous), *al-ʿAẓīm* (the Almighty)... So, he finds comfort in *al-Bāri* (the Creator), and loves *al-ʿAẓīm* (the Almighty) and feels close to *al-ʿAlīm* (the All-Knowing).

The feeling that Allah is close to His slave brings comfort and the joy of knowing that one is under His care.

﴿وَإِذَا سَأَلَكَ عِبَادِى عَنِّى فَإِنِّى قَرِيبٌ أُجِيبُ دَعْوَةَ ٱلدَّاعِ إِذَا دَعَانِ ... ﴾ (٨٦)   (سورة البَقَرَة: ١٨٦)

❨And when My slaves ask you [O' Muhammad] concerning Me, [then answer them], I am indeed near [to them by My Knowledge]. I respond to the invocations of the supplicant when he calls on Me...❩

(Qur'an 2: 186)

But finding comfort in Allah does not just happen without hard work and striving for it. It is the fruit of obedience, the result of love. Whoever obeys Allah and follows His commands and avoids that which He has forbidden and loves Him sincerely, will find joy and comfort in being close to Him.

"Real beauty lies in beautiful behaviour, manners and mind."

"I urge you to be kind to women." *(Hadith)*

10
She of the Two Girdles lived two lives

Asmā' bint Abi Bakr, *Dhāt an-Niṭāqayn* (she of the Two Girdles) set a good and vivid example of patience at times of hardship and intense deprivation, and of keenness to obey one's husband and striving to please him. It is narrated in a *ṣaḥīḥ* hadith that she said:

"When az-Zubayr married me, he had nothing except his horse, which I used to look after and feed, and I used to crush date stones for his camel that drew water. I used to bring water and bake dough too. One day I was bringing the date stones from the land of az-Zubayr that the Messenger of Allah (Blessings and Peace be upon him) had allocated to him and I met the Messenger of Allah (Blessings and Peace be upon him) and with him was a group of people. The Messenger (Blessings and Peace be upon him) called me and made his camel kneel down so that I could ride behind him, but I felt shy and remembered az-Zubayr and his sense of *gheerah* (pride or protective jealousy). So he went on, and when I came to az-Zubayr I told him what had happened. He said: 'By Allah, your carrying the date-stones is harder for me than your riding with him.' Then after that Abu Bakr sent me a servant who relieved me of looking after the horse, and it was as if I had been set free (from slavery)."

After all this patience, blessings came along and overwhelmed her and her husband, but she did not lose her balance as a result of riches, rather, she was very generous and did not store anything for the future. When she fell sick, she would wait until she got better then she would set all her slaves free. And she told her daughters and her family: "Spend and give in charity; do not wait until you have something extra."

"Life is beautiful for the believers, the Hereafter is beloved to the pious; they are the only happy ones."

Chapter 11

Chapter 11

⟨... And be not distressed because of what they plot...⟩

(Qur'an 16: 127)

1
Who is the dearest beloved?

Love him more than all others.

Have you ever asked yourself how much you love the Messenger of Allah (Blessings and Peace be upon him)? Do you know what the sign of that love is? It is doing all that the Messenger of Allah enjoined and avoiding all that he forbade. Look again at your emotions and direct them, firstly, towards love of Allah, then love of the one by means of whom Allah saved us from misguidance. Remember, if you want your position in Paradise to be lofty, the hadith of the Messenger (Blessings and Peace be upon him): *"A person will be with the one whom he loves."* But one of the first signs and manifestations of that love is doing what he (bpuh) commanded. How can anyone claim to love him when he does the opposite of what he enjoined and does not follow his guidance and adhere to his path? Pick up a book of *Sīrah* (the Prophet's biography) and read it; see for yourself how great his attitude was, how noble and kind the way he spoke, how loving his approach, how he feared Allah and shunned this world. Change your attitude and make it more like his.

"The wives of Nūḥ and Lūṭ betrayed their husbands (by rejecting their teachings), so they became insignificant before Allah. But Āsiyah and Maryam believed, so they were honoured."

❨... I am indeed near [to them by My Knowledge]. I respond to
the invocations of the supplicant when he calls on Me...❩

(Qur'an 2: 186)

2

Happiness has nothing to do with richness or poverty

Bernard Shaw said:

"I cannot say that I have ever really tasted poverty. Before I was
ever able to earn a living by means of my pen, I had access to a
huge library, the public library of the British Museum, and the best
of art exhibits near Trafalgar Square. What could I have done with
money? Smoke cigars? But I do not smoke. Drink champagne?
But I do not drink. Buy thirty suits in the latest fashion? But then I
would quickly be invited to dinner in palaces by those whom I try
to avoid as much as possible. Buy horses? But they are dangerous.
Cars? But they annoy me. Now I have enough money to buy all of
these things, but I only buy what I used to buy when I was poor.
My happiness is in the same things that used to help me when I
was poor: a book to read, a painting to ponder over, an idea to
write. On the other hand, I have a fertile imagination and I cannot
remember needing anything more than to lie on my back and
imagine myself the way I like, doing whatever I want in my
imagination. So, of what use to me are the miserable luxuries that
are sold in Bond Street?"

"Make your house a paradise of
tranquility, not a noisy playground,
for quietness is a blessing."

《... My Lord! Build for me a home near You in Paradise...》

(Qur'an 66: 11)

3
Is not Allah more deserving of thanks than anyone else?

Thanking Allah, the All-Merciful, is the best and easiest prescription for happiness and calming the nerves, because when you thank your Lord, you remember the blessings that He has bestowed upon you, and you appreciate the blessings that you are enjoying. One of the righteous *salaf* (predecessors) used to say:

"If you want to know the blessing that Allah has bestowed upon you, close your eyes." Look at how He has blessed you with hearing, sight, reason, religious commitment, children, provision, a good life. Some women think little of the blessings that they enjoy, but if they looked at others who are poor, destitute, sick, homeless or traumatized, they would praise Allah for the blessings that they have, even if they lived in a tent of goat hair or a mud hut or beneath a tree in the desert. Praise Allah, the Exalted, for these blessings and compare yourself with those who are afflicted with physical or mental health problems, or who cannot hear, or who have lost their children, for there are many such women in this world.

"Comfort those who have lost their children with a kind word, and wipe away the tears of the poor with charity."

"It is impossible for the status quo to remain as it is."

4
The happy woman makes those around her happy, too

Orizon Sweet said:

Napoleon was very fortunate to marry the Empress Josephine before he took high command and was faced with the challenges of conquest. Her gentle ways and sweet personality were more effective than the sincerity of dozens of men in earning him the loyalty of his supporters. She used to spread happiness around herself and never used direct commands, even to servants. She herself explained that clearly when she said to one of her friends: "There is no context in which I can say 'I want' except when I say that I want everyone around me to be happy." It is as if the English poet was referring to her when he said:

"She passed by the road on a happy morning and
the glory of the morning spread throughout the day."

The truth is, my friend, that kindness spreads happiness among us and among those around us, even inanimate objects. Kindness has an intangible beauty that knows no boundary. For man, this is like beauty in a woman, and for woman this increases her beauty manifold.

"Is she happy who shows her beauty
to the dogs of mankind and displays
her charms to the wolves of them?"

"Acknowledge Allah at times of ease,
He will help you at times of hardship."

5
Be content, for everything happens by the will and decree of Allah

One of the things that Dale Carnegie mentions instead of belief in the divine will and decree (*al-qaḍā' wal-qadar*) is that man expects the one who is stricken by a calamity to freeze and not react to that calamity, like a buffalo or a tree trunk. He may be excused for that, because he did not find out the remedy that we Muslims have access to. Listen to him when he said:

"Once I refused to accept something inevitable with which I was faced, but I was a fool. I objected, went mad, got angry, and turned my nights into a hell of insomnia. After a year of psychological torment, I gave in to the inevitable; I had known from the outset that there was no way to change it and it would have been more appropriate if I had done what the poet Walt Whitman suggests:

'How much better it is to face darkness, storms, hunger, calamities, blame and rebuke as animals and tree trunks do.'

I spent twelve years of my life with cattle, and I never saw a cow get upset because the grazing land was on fire, or because it was dry due to lack of rain, or because her mate the bull was approaching another cow. Animals always face darkness, storms and starvation in a calm and tranquil manner; it is very rare for an animal to have a nervous breakdown or a stomach ulcer!"

"Remember success and other joyful

things, forget calamities and
disturbing things."

❴... And Allah is Ever All-Sufficient as a Disposer of affairs.❵

(Qur'an 4: 81)

6
Umm 'Amārah speaks

Nusaybah bint Ka'b (Umm 'Amārah) (may Allah be pleased with her) narrated the story of the day of *Uḥud*. She said:

"I went out at the beginning of the day to see what the people were doing. I had a waterskin with me in which there was water. I came to the Messenger of Allah (Blessings and Peace be upon him), who was with a number of his Companions, and the Muslims were winning. When the battle turned against the Muslims, I came closer to the Messenger of Allah and started to fight, striking blows with a sword and shooting arrows, until I was wounded. When the people scattered and left the Messenger of Allah, Ibn Qumay'ah came and said, 'Show me where Muhammad is; may I not live if I let him live!' I confronted him, along with Muṣ'ab ibn 'Umayr, and he dealt me this blow on my shoulder. I struck him many times but the enemy of Allah had two layers of armour."

This is Umm 'Amārah, of whom the Messenger of Allah (Blessings and Peace be upon him) said: "*I did not turn to my right or my left on the day of Uḥud but I saw her fighting to defend me.*"

"Beware of noise, for it causes
exhaustion; and beware of insults,
for they imply a torment."

*"Nine-tenths of a good attitude consist
of overlooking mistakes."*

7
Kindness to others
washes away grief

There are many hadiths of the Messenger of Allah (Blessings and Peace be upon him) in the context of generosity of women, either encouraging women to give charity, praising them for their generosity, speaking highly of their cheer-ful selflessness towards guests, friends and loved ones. The mother of the believers 'Ā'ishah (may Allah be pleased with her) narrated that, *"They slaughtered a sheep. The Messenger of Allah asked, 'What is left of it?' She said: 'There is nothing left but the shoulder.' The Prophet said: 'Everything is left but the shoulder.'"*

The Prophet (Blessings and Peace be upon him) was explaining to his household that the reward for what they had given away would remain on the Day of Resurrection, and that whatever was left and eaten by them in this world would not bring a reward that would benefit them in the Hereafter. This is a wise hint that encourages us to give charity, seeking thereby the pleasure of Allah, the All-Glorious.

Asmā', the sister of 'Ā'ishah, was advised by the Prophet (Blessings and Peace be upon him) to give charity so that Allah would give her more of His bounty. She said: "The Messenger of Allah said to me: *'Do not withhold charity lest Allah would withhold (provision) from you.'*"

"As long as night has an end, pain will cease, crises will pass and hardship will disappear."

"Blessing is a bride whose dowry is gratitude."

8
Turn your losses into gains

Wise words of advice:

Do not despair if your feet stumble and you fall into a big hole. You will come out of it stronger than before. And Allah, the Almighty, is with those who are patient.

Do not grieve if you receive a fatal arrow from one of those who are closest to your heart, for you will find someone to pull out the arrow, treat the wound and bring back to you life and smile.

Do not stand for too long looking at the ruins, especially if they are inhabited by bats, and ghosts have found their way to them. Rather, look for the sound of a birdsong heralding the coming of a new dawn.

Do not look at papers whose colour has changed and whose writing has faded, whose lines wander between pain and loneliness. You will find that these lines are not the best things that you have written and these papers are not the last thing you will ever write. You should differentiate between one who will read these lines and one who will throw them to the wind, for they are not merely beautiful words; they are the feelings of a heart that has lived these lines, letter by letter, the pulse of one who took them as a dream and felt the pain of their fire. Do not be like the heron, which sings its most beautiful song when it is bleeding. Nothing in this world deserves even one drop of your blood.

"He who sows the wind, reaps the storm."

◀[Delicate and pure] as if they were [dedicate]
eggs [well] preserved▶ *(Qur'an 37: 49)*

9
Sincerity is very precious;
where are the sincere ones?

One of those who have a great deal of knowledge about
Allah, submit to His will and accept His decree was the Prophet of
Allah Ayyūb (may Allah's peace be upon him). He was tested and
afflicted with regard to his physical health, his wealth and his
children, until there was not a patch in his body in the size of a
needle that remained sound, except for his heart. He had no
worldly means to help him apart from his wife, who remained
loyal to him because of her faith in Allah and His Messenger (may
Allah's peace be upon him). She used to work as a servant in order
to earn money, and she fed him and took care of him for nearly
eighteen years, never leaving him morning or evening except
when she went to serve people, then she would come back to him.
This difficult state of affairs lasted for a long time until the
appointed hour came, he beseeched the Lord of the Worlds, the
God of the Messengers, the most Merciful of those who show
mercy, calling upon Him and saying:

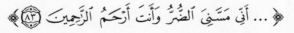

(سورة الأنبياء: ٨٣)

◀... Verily, distress has seized me, and You are the
Most Merciful of all those who show mercy.▶

(Qur'an 21: 83)

Allah, the All-Gracious, All-Merciful, answered his prayer. He commanded him to get up straight away and to strike the ground with his foot. He did so, and Allah caused a spring to gush forth, then He commanded him to bathe in it, and all the sickness in his body disappeared. Then He commanded him to strike the ground in another spot, which caused another spring to gush forth. He commanded him to drink from it, and all the sickness inside him disappeared, and he became healthy and whole, both inwardly and outwardly. All of that was the fruit of patience and the result of seeking reward from Allah and accepting His Will.

> "Man may regret speaking, but he will never regret silence."

"Woman is the source of happiness."

10
Be serious, be serious...

You should be serious in all your affairs, in raising your children, persisting in doing useful deeds, reading good books, reading Qur'an and praying with proper focus and humility, remembering Allah with proper presence of mind, giving charity, keeping your house tidy, organizing your bookshelves... By doing such serious things you will put an end to grief and worry.

Look at some of the disbelieving women, let alone the believing women, and how they are distinguished by their serious attitude towards life, despite their disbelief and deviance from the straight path. Look at the former prime minister of Israel, the dead Golda Meir. She wrote memoirs in which she described her seriousness in organizing the army and her attitude towards the wars with the Arabs. Hardly any of the men of her own race could match her, even though she was a *kāfirah* (a female disbeliever) and an enemy of Allah.

"Happiness is not some kind of magic; if it were, it would be of no value."

Chapter 12

Chapter 12

⟪Truly, Allah is with those who fear Him [keep their duty unto Him], and those who are *Muḥsinūn* [good-doers].⟫

(Qur'an 16: 128)

1
Take a brave stance when you check yourself

Ask yourself these questions and answer wisely:

— Do you know that you are travelling on a journey from which there will be no return? Have you prepared yourself for this journey?

— Have you taken provision from this transient world in the form of righteous deeds to give you comfort and soothe your loneliness in the grave?

— How old are you? How long will you live? Don't you know that for every beginning there is an end and the end will be either Paradise or Hell?

— Have you imagined how it will be if the angels come down from heaven to take your soul while you are heedless and having fun?

— Have you imagined that day, the last hour in your life, the hour when you leave your family and children, your nearest and dearest? That is death with all its agonies and the intense pain of the soul's departure. That is death...

— After your soul has departed your body and you are taken to be washed and shrouded, then taken to the mosque for the funeral prayer to be offered for you, then you are carried on the shoulders of men... where are you being taken? To the grave, to the first stage of the Hereafter. Will it be one of the gardens of Paradise or one of the ditches of Hell?

"Learn from your failure."

❨And He it is Who sends down the rain
after they have despaired...❩

(Qur'an 42: 28)

2
Beware!

Beware of imitating disbelieving and immoral women or men. According to the hadith: *"Allah has cursed the men who imitate women and the women who imitate men."* Beware of everything that angers the Lord, some of which are forbidden in hadith, such as imitating men, being alone with a non-*maḥram* man, travelling without a *maḥram*, losing one's modesty, not dressing properly, forgetting one's Lord. All of these are shameful deeds which cause distress in the heart and darkness in this world and in the Hereafter. This is something that has become common and widespread among Muslim women, except those on whom Allah, the All-Merciful, has mercy.

"In order to be beautiful, your thoughts should be so."

❨... Our Lord! Forgive us our sins
and the excess in our affairs...❩

(Qur'an 3: 147)

3
Being grateful to the beneficent is a duty

(Al-Khayzarān) was a slave woman whom the caliph al-Mahdi bought from the slave-trader, then he set her free and married her. He did as she wished and appointed two sons of hers to be her heirs. But when she got angry with him, she would say to his face: "I have never seen anything good from you!"

(Al-Barmakiyyah) was another slave woman who was bought and sold. Then she was bought by al-Mu'tamid ibn 'Abbād, the king of Morocco. He freed her and made her a queen. When she saw the slave girls playing with mud, she became nostalgic and wanted to play with mud like them. The king ordered that a huge amount of perfume be prepared for her, in the form of mud, so that she could play with it. But when she got angry with him she said to him: "I have never seen anything good from you!" He would simply smile and say to her: "Not even the day of the mud?" Then she would get embarrassed...

It is the nature of women — except a few — to forget whatever favours have been done to them when a husband forgets or falls short in his treatment of them. It says in the hadith: *"O' woman, give in charity, for I have seen that you form the majority of the inhabitants of Hell."* They said: "Why, O' Messenger of Allah?" He (Blessings and Peace be upon him) said: *"You are quick to curse, you slander a great deal and you are ungrateful to a kind companion."*

The Prophet (Blessings and Peace be upon him) also said: *"I was shown Hell and most of its inhabitants were women, because they are ungrateful to a kind companion and are ungrateful for kind treatment. If you treat one of them kindly for a lifetime, then she sees something (she dislikes) from you, she will say, I have never seen anything good from you!"* If a man knew the nature of women, he would not get angry, worried or tense if a woman sometimes shows ingratitude towards him or claims that she had never seen anything good from him, even though he has done a great deal for her.

"The successful woman is supplicated for, praised by her husband, loved by her neighbours and respected by her friends."

"My mercy prevails over My wrath."

(Hadith qudsi)

4

The soul deserves more care than the body

When 'Umar ibn 'Abd al-'Azīz was caliph, he ordered a man to buy him a garment for eight dirhams. The man bought it and brought it to him. 'Umar placed his hand on it and said: "How lovely and soft it is!" The man who had brought it smiled, and 'Umar asked him, "Why are you smiling?" He said: "Because, O' *Amīr al-Mu'minīn* (Leader of Believers), before you became caliph, you ordered me to buy a silk cloak for you, and I bought it for one thousand dirhams, but you put your hand on it and said, 'How rough it is!' Today you find an eight-dirham garment soft."

'Umar said: "I don't think that a man who buys a garment for one-thousand dirhams fears Allah." Then he said: "I have an ambitious soul. Every time it attains one position, it looks for something higher. I became governor, then I wanted to become caliph. Now I have become caliph, and my soul is longing for something greater than that, namely Paradise."

"Judging people is not our responsibility. It is *not our duty to think of punishing others.*"

"Keep your duty to Allah and
He will take care of you."

5
Keep busy with the present rather than the past or future

What is the point in slapping your cheeks or rending your garment in sorrow over something you missed or some calamity that befell you? What is the point in focusing your thoughts and feelings on some incident that has passed so as to increase your pain and make you fall apart?

If it were possible to reach into the past and change its events which we did not like, and alter them the way we like, then going back to the past would be essential. We would all rush to go back and erase the things we regretted doing and increase our share of good fortune. But that is impossible, so it is better for us to focus our efforts on what will help us get on with our lives, for that is our only means of compensation.

This is what the Qur'an drew attention to after *Uḥud* (a battle named after a mountain in Madīnah), when Allah said to those who were weeping for the slain and regretting going out to the battlefield:

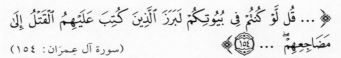

(سورة آل عِمرَان: ١٥٤)

❰... Say: 'Even if you had remained in your homes, those for whom death was decreed would certainly have gone forth to the place of their death'...❱

(Qur'an 3: 154)

"Be certain that happiness is like a planted flower that has not yet blossomed, but it is certain to appear."

❨But whosoever turns away from My remembrance [i.e.
neither believes in this Qur'an nor acts on its
teachings] verily, for him is a life of hardship...❩

(Qur'an 20: 124)

6
Calamities are means of attaining desires

It is narrated that Umm al-'Alā' (may Allah be pleased with
her) said: "The Messenger of Allah (Blessings and Peace be upon
him) visited me when I was sick and said: *'Be of good cheer, O'
Umm al-'Alā', for by means of a Muslim's sickness Allah takes
away his sin as the fire takes away the dross of silver.'*"

This does not mean that we should breed germs in our
bodies or be careless about seeking medical treatment on the basis
that sickness erases sin. Rather, we should seek healing and cure,
whilst still bearing the sickness with patience and seeking reward
for the pain from Allah. We should regard it as a means of storing
up good deeds in our record. This is the lesson that this righteous
woman is teaching us.

Women should bear with patience the loss of beloved ones
such as their husbands and children. In the hadith it says: *"Allah
will not be pleased to give his believing slave any reward less than
Paradise, if a dear one among the people of the world is taken
from him and he accepts that with patience and seeks reward from
Allah."*

If a woman loses her husband, it means that Allah has taken back His slave, and He is more entitled to that. If the woman says, "My husband!" or "My son!" the Creator says, "My slave, and I have more right to him than anyone else." A husband is a loan, a child is a loan, a brother is a loan, a father is a loan, a wife is a loan.

"Avoid slander as you would avoid the plague."

"Those who show mercy will be shown mercy
by the Most Merciful."

(Hadith)

7
Show mercy to those who are on earth and the One Who is in heaven will show mercy to you

The mercy of a mother to her children is explained very clearly in the hadiths of the Messenger of Allah (Blessings and Peace be upon him). It is the ideal of love and compassion, the wellspring of pity and compassion which the Prophet (Blessings and Peace be upon him) presented as a vivid example to explain the mercy of Allah, the Almighty, All-Merciful, to His slaves. "Umar ibn al-Khaṭṭāb (may Allah be pleased with him) narrated that some female prisoners were brought to the Messenger of Allah, and he saw a woman searching frantically. When she found a child, she hugged him to her chest and began to breastfeed him. The Messenger of Allah (Blessings and Peace be upon him) said: *"Do you think that this woman could throw her child into the fire?"* They said: *"No, by Allah."* He said: *"Allah is more merciful to His slaves than this woman to her child."*

This was a woman who was taken captive, was upset and full of grief. She had been a sovereign among her household, free under the care of the men of her tribe, obeyed in the house of her husband. Her captivity made her a slave to be ordered. She was in a situation where any person would forget what was going on around him, and his heart would be filled with pain, but that did not distract her from caring for her child, the apple of her eye. She searched high and low until she found him, then she clasped him to her breast. Such a woman would never allow her child to suffer any hurt, no matter how slight, and she would defend him against any harm, no matter how insignificant. She would sacrifice herself to protect him.

> "Foul tongues cause more trouble to their owners than to their victims."

"Showing gratitude to Allah protects one from His wrath."

8
The beautiful world is seen only by optimists

If winter has closed the doors of your house and mountains of snow have besieged you in all directions, then look forward to the coming of spring and open your windows to a breath of fresh air. Look far ahead, and see the flocks of birds starting to sing again. You will see the sun shining its golden rays on the branches to give you a new life, a new dream and a new heart. Do not travel to the desert looking for beautiful trees, for you will never find there anything but loneliness. Look at the hundreds of trees that offer you shade and fruits and the delightful singing of birds sheltering in them.

Do not try to look at what happened yesterday and what you lost, for in life, when a leaf falls it will never come back, but with each new spring new leaves will grow. Look at the canopy of leaves between you and the sky, and forget about the leaves that have fallen to the ground and have become part of the earth.

Since the past is past, you have today ahead of you, and if today is going to gather its leaves and depart, then you have tomorrow. Do not grieve for yesterday, for it will never return. Do not regret today, for it is leaving. Dream, instead, about the shining sun in beautiful tomorrow.

> "It is impossible to imagine the scope of disease caused by exchanging hurtful words."

"Women are the twin halves of men."

(Hadith)

9
Acknowledge Allah at times of ease and He will help you at times of hardship

When Prophet Yūnus (may Allah's peace be upon him) was filled with distress in the belly of the whale, covered by those vast layers of darkness — the darkness of the sea, the darkness of the whale's belly and the darkness of the night — when he was worried and anxious, he turned to Allah, the Almighty, All-Merciful, the One Who helps the depressed and rescues the distressed; the One Whose mercy is immense, the One Who accepts repentance, then he spoke those precious words:

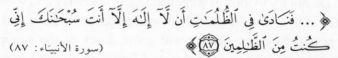

(سورة الأنبياء : ٨٧)

❴... But he called out through the darkness [saying]: 'Lā ilāha illa Anta [none has the right to be worshipped but You (O' Allah)], Glorified [and Exalted] are You [above all that (evil) they associate with You]! Truly, I have been of the wrongdoers.'❵

(Qur'an 21: 87)

And the response came swiftly, as Allah, the Exalted, says:

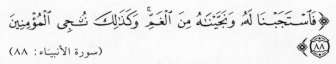

❮So We answered his call, and delivered him from the distress. And thus We do deliver the believers [who believe in the Oneness of Allah, abstain from evil and work righteousness].❯   *(Qur'an 21: 88)*

Allah inspired the whale to throw Yūnus out in a deserted area. He came up onto the shore sick and weak, but Allah took care of him and bestowed His mercy upon him. He caused a kind of squash plant with broad leaves to grow over him. His health was restored and signs of life began to appear in him. This is how it is for the one who acknowledges Allah at times of ease: He helps him at times of hardship.

> **"You do not deserve to lead yourself until you deserve to lead your life."**

"Poor is the man who does not have a wife."

10
The woman with the highest dowry in the world

Abu Ṭalḥah proposed marriage to Umm Sulaym bint Milḥān, and he offered her a valuable dowry, but to his astonishment she refused all that with pride, saying: "I cannot marry a *mushrik* (polytheist). Do you not know, O' Abu Ṭalḥah, that your gods were carved by the slave of such and such a family, and if you were to set them on fire they would burn!"

Abu Ṭalḥah was deeply distressed, and he went away hardly believing what he had seen and heard. But his sincere love brought him back the next day, offering a greater and more valuable dowry in the hope that this would soften her heart and make her accept. But with the utmost grace and good manners, she told him: "A man like you is not to be rejected, O' Abu Ṭalḥah, but you are a *kāfir* (disbeliever) and I am a Muslim woman. It is not right for me to marry you." He said: "I will give you the yellow and the white (gold and silver)." She said, "I want neither yellow nor white, I want you to become Muslim." He said: "Who can I talk to about that?" She said: "Talk to the Messenger of Allah." So he set off to look for the Prophet (Blessings and Peace be upon him), who was sitting with a number of his Companions. When he saw the Prophet he said: "Abu Ṭalḥah has come to you with the light of Islam in his eyes." He came and told the Prophet what Umm Sulaym had said, and he married her to him on that basis.

This woman is a fine example for anyone who is seeking glory and virtue. Look at how her way of life manifested signs of nobility and faith, and how great her reward will be from Allah. Look at the good memory she left behind, so that people remember her and praise her. She has earned a great and blessed reward, because she was sincere towards her Lord, towards herself and towards other people.

$$ \text{﴿ ... هَٰذَا يَوْمُ يَنفَعُ ٱلصَّٰدِقِينَ صِدْقُهُمْ ... ﴾} $$

(سورة المَائدة: ١١٩)

❨... This is a Day on which the truthful will profit from their truthfulness...❩   *(Qur'an 5: 119)*

So she received glad tidings of Paradise, to abide therein forever with the joy of being among the winners.

> "You should smile if you want others to smile at you."

Chapter 13

《... And bear with patience whatever befalls you...》

(Qur'an 31: 17)

1
The keys to victory

— The key to glory: Obedience to Allah and His Messenger (Blessings and Peace be upon him)

— The key to provision: Striving hard whilst praying for forgiveness and fearing Allah, the Exalted

— The key to Paradise: *Tawḥīd* (Monotheism)

— The key to faith: Pondering the signs and creation of Allah

— The key to righteousness: Sincerity

— The key to a spiritual life: Studying the Qur'an, beseeching Allah in the hours before dawn, and giving up sin

— The key to knowledge: Asking the right questions and listening attentively

— The key to victory: Patience

— The key to success: Fearing Allah (piety)

— The key to getting more: Gratitude

— The key to longing for the Hereafter: Disinterest in worldly gains

— The key to a response: *Du'ā'* (supplication)

"A smile is like a ray of sunshine."

《Our Lord!... grant us mercy from You...》

(Qur'an 3: 8)

2
After suffering comes
the joy of victory

In a letter to her mother after returning from her honeymoon, a wife wrote to her mother:

Dear Mother, today I came home to my house, to the little nest that my husband had prepared for me, after our honeymoon. I wish that you were nearby, so that I could tell you all about my new life with my husband. He is a good man and he loves me, and I love him and do everything I can to please him. You may rest assured that I remembered all your advice and acted upon it. I still remember every word... every letter you told me and whispered in my ear when you hugged me to your breast on my wedding night.

I see life through the lens of what I heard from you. You have been a great example to me. I have no other goal except to do what you did for my dear father and for us when we were children. You gave us all your love and compassion, you taught us the meaning of life and how to live. You sowed the seeds of love in our hearts with your own hand.

I can hear the key in the door; it must be my husband. He wants to read my letter to you, he wants to know what I have written to my mother. He wants to join me in these happy moments that I have spent with you in spirit and in thoughts. He is asking me to give him the pen and spare him some space to write to you. My love to you, to my father and my brothers and sisters.

"A smile does not cost anything, but
it gives a great deal."

❝... Our Lord! Accept [this service] from us. Verily,
You are the All-Hearing, the All-Knowing.❞

(Qur'an 2: 127)

3
Anxiety exhausts the body and the mind

One of the worst consequences of anxiety is that it makes us unable to focus. When we are anxious our mind is scattered, but if we force ourselves to confront the worst-case scenario, we put ourselves in a position where we can focus our minds on the heart (core) of the matter.

We cannot be enthusiastic about an exciting task and feel worry at the same time; one of them will chase away the other.

When you feel anxious about something in the present, go back to the worst case of anxiety that you can remember. Thus, you will deal with your anxiety in two ways instead of one. The episode in the past was worse, but you coped with it, so you will be able to deal with the present problem which is less intense; one could say that there is nothing worse than the past episode, but you got through it successfully. If you faced that crisis and came through it safely, then how less serious and less dangerous the current problem is.

Anxiety is more likely to overwhelm you at times when you are not active, when your imagination runs wild and thinks of all possible scenarios. The remedy for that is to keep yourself busy with something useful.

"Trivial things may push wise people to the brink of insanity."

"Life is no more than minutes and seconds."

4

Your loved job is the secret of your happiness

A genius in any field is overwhelmingly and irresistibly attracted to the field for which Allah, the Exalted, created him and in which He gave him the potential to be innovative and creative. Even if he complains about the backlog in that field, it is still the only area that he can work in with contentment and enjoyment, no matter what difficulties he encounters, how small the remuneration or how much he sighs and wishes he could do something more lucrative. Regardless of how much he complains about the poverty caused by this profession, it is still giving him contentment and bringing out the best in him.

"Man finds happiness in a word that comes from the lips of a woman."

❨And when I am ill, it is He Who cures me...❩ *(Qur'an 26: 80)*

5
Strength is in the spirit, not in the body

A Christian woman knew nothing in life but poverty, hunger and sickness. Her husband died shortly after they were married and her second husband left her and ran off with another woman, after which he was found dead in a filthy hovel. She had one son. But because of poverty and sickness, she found herself forced to give him up when he was four years old.

The turning point in her life came when she was walking through the city streets one day and she slipped and fell on a patch of icy ground. She fell into coma for a long time, and sustained a spinal injury because of her fall. The doctors expected her either to die soon, or to be completely paralyzed for life.

Whilst she was lying in her hospital bed, she opened the Holy Book and was inspired by Divine care — as she put it — to read these words from the Gospel of Matthew:

"Some men brought to him [to 'Īsā (Peace be upon him)] a paralytic, lying on a mat... Then he said to the paralytic: 'Get up, take your mat and go home.' And the man got up and went home." (Matthew 9:2, 6-7)

These words gave her strong faith and motivated her so much that she got up from the bed and started to walk about the room. This experience paved the way for this paralyzed woman to treat herself and bring healing to others.

Dale Carnegie said: "This is the experience that enabled Mary Baker Eddie to become the missioner of a new religion[2], which is perhaps the only religion to have been founded by a woman."

And you, O' Muslim woman, what have you done?

> "The strongest fortress is a righteous woman."

---

[2] It should be noted that the point here is not to praise or condone that "new religion", for there is to be no new revelation or Prophet after Muhammad (Blessings and Peace be upon him) brought the Qur'ān and the message of Islam. Rather the author's point here is to praise a woman who rose above adversity and made a difference in the life of others. (Translator)

"Contentment is an inexhaustible treasure."

6

A great woman turns a hell of calamity into a paradise

The great *Ṣaḥābiyah* (a female Companion of the Prophet), Umm Sulaym, the wife of Abu Ṭalḥah, set a great example of patience at losing a child, and Allah, the Almighty, All-Merciful, compensated her greatly.

Anas (may Allah be pleased with him) said: A son of Abu Ṭalḥah (may Allah be pleased with him) was sick. Abu Ṭalḥah went out, and the boy passed away. When Abu Ṭalḥah came back, he said: "How is my son?" Umm Sulaym, the mother of the boy, said: "He is better than he was." Then she brought him his dinner and he ate, then he was intimate with her. When that was over, she said: "Bury the boy." The following morning, Abu Ṭalḥah came to the Messenger of Allah (Blessings and Peace be upon him) and told him what had happened. *He (the Prophet) asked: "Were you intimate last night?" He said: "Yes." The Prophet said: "O' Allah, bless them." She gave birth to a boy, and Abu Ṭalḥah said to me (Anas): "Take him to the Prophet," and he sent some dates with him. The Prophet said: "Have you brought something with him?" I said: "Yes, dates." The Prophet took some and chewed them, then he took some from his mouth and placed it in the infant's mouth, then he named him 'Abdullāh.*

"Nothing raises the status of a woman like chastity."

*"Give glad tidings to the night of a dawn
that is sure to come."*

7
Be patient to be victorious

It is narrated that Umm ar-Rubay' bint al-Barā', the mother of Hārithah ibn Surāqah who was killed in the battle of Badr, came to the Prophet (Blessings and Peace be upon him) hoping to hear something from him about her martyred son that would soothe her heart. She said: *"O' Messenger of Allah, will you not tell me about Hārithah? If he is in Paradise, I will bear it with patience, but if it is otherwise, then I will weep a great deal for him."* He said: *"O' mother of Hārithah, there are many gardens in Paradise and your son has attained the highest Firdaws (garden)."*

Losing a child is a grievous matter that breaks one's heart and tears one apart. This woman told the Prophet (Blessings and Peace be upon him) that if her son was in Paradise, she would meet him again *"in shā' Allah* (if Allah Wills). Thus, she could bear the separation with patience, and that raised her status and his in Paradise. But if that was not the case, then she would weep bitterly for him, like one who has lost a dear one forever. This was all that she could do, because she was a compassionate and loving mother who had lost her child, but she bore that with patience and sought reward from Allah, the All-Merciful.

"If a beautiful woman is a jewel, a
righteous woman is a treasure."

"Woman is a sun that does not set."

8

In hardships, we have no refuge except Allah Alone

When anxiety rears its head, worries come along and a crisis overwhelms man, making him feel that there is no way out and he is helpless, he cries out, "O' Allah, O' Allah... *Lā ilāha illallah al-'Aẓīm al-Ḥalīm; Lā ilāha illallah Rabb al-'arsh al-'aẓīm; Lā ilāha illallah Rabb as-samāwāti wa Rabb al-arḍ wa Rabb al-'arsh al-karīm* (There is no god except Allah, the Almighty, the Forbearing; there is no god but Allah, Lord of the mighty Throne; there is no god but Allah, Lord of the heavens, Lord of the earth and Lord of the noble Throne). Then his worry is dispelled and he is relieved of distress.

﴿فَٱسْتَجَبْنَا لَهُۥ وَنَجَّيْنَٰهُ مِنَ ٱلْغَمِّ ۚ وَكَذَٰلِكَ نُـۨجِى ٱلْمُؤْمِنِينَ ۝﴾

(سورة الأنبياء: ٨٨)

❁So We answered his call, and delivered him from the distress. And thus We do deliver the believers.❁

(Qur'an 21: 88)

﴿وَمَا بِكُم مِّن نِّعْمَةٍ فَمِنَ ٱللَّهِ ۖ ثُمَّ إِذَا مَسَّكُمُ ٱلضُّرُّ فَإِلَيْهِ تَجْـَٔرُونَ ۝﴾

(سورة النحل: ٥٣)

❁And whatever of blessings and good things you have, it is from Allah. Then, when harm touches you, unto Him you cry aloud for help.❁ *(Qur'an 16: 53)*

When sickness gets worse and a person's body becomes weak, he turns pale and feels helpless, and the doctors are unable to do anything, and he is filled with despair, his hands tremble and he feels palpitations in his heart, then the sick one turns to the Almighty and says, O' Allah, O' Allah. Then his sickness is relieved and healing begins, and his prayer is answered:

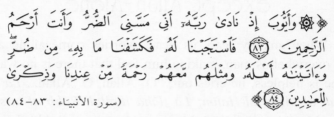

(سورة الأنبياء: ٨٣-٨٤)

◉And [remember] Ayyūb [Job], when he cried to his Lord: "Verily, distress has seized me, and You are the Most Merciful of all those who show mercy." So We answered his call, and We removed the distress that was on him, and We restored his family to him [that he had lost] and the like thereof along with them as a mercy from Ourselves and a Reminder for all those who worship Us.◉   *(Qur'an 21: 83-84)*

"The best thing a man can have is a faithful wife."

"Women are fragile like bottles: handle with care."

9
Is not He (better than your gods) Who responds to the distressed one, when he calls on Him?

By His generosity, the Creator does not let down the one who puts his hope in Him, and He does not neglect the one who calls on Him. According to a person's need and how much he humbles himself before Him and turns to Him, He will answer his prayers and grant him a way out. Indeed, by His grace, He even answers the prayers of non-Muslim people when they turn to Him in desperation and humble themselves before Him, trusting His kindness and hoping for His generosity. He answers their call and relieves their distress by His kindness, to make them love Him, so that they might believe, but many people forget His favours and are ungrateful for His kindness. Allah, the Almighty, says:

﴿فَإِذَا رَكِبُوا۟ فِى ٱلْفُلْكِ دَعَوُا۟ ٱللَّهَ مُخْلِصِينَ لَهُ ٱلدِّينَ فَلَمَّا نَجَّىٰهُمْ إِلَى ٱلْبَرِّ إِذَا هُمْ يُشْرِكُونَ ۝﴾   (سورة العَنكبوت: ٦٥)

❨And when they embark on a ship, they invoke Allah, making their Faith pure for Him only: but when He brings them safely to land, behold, they give a share of their worship to others.❩   *(Qur'an 29: 65)*

Allah reminds His slaves that He is the One Who answers the call of the distressed one when he calls on Him. This is one of the signs of His divinity and proof of His Oneness, but people understand little.

$$﴿أَمَّن يُجِيبُ ٱلْمُضْطَرَّ إِذَا دَعَاهُ وَيَكْشِفُ ٱلسُّوٓءَ وَيَجْعَلُكُمْ خُلَفَآءَ ٱلْأَرْضِ أَءِلَٰهٌ مَّعَ ٱللَّهِ قَلِيلًا مَّا تَذَكَّرُونَ ۝﴾$$

(سورة النَّمل: ٦٢)

﴿Is not He [better than your gods] Who responds to the distressed one, when he calls on Him, and Who removes the evil, and makes you inheritors of the earth, [generations after generations]? Is there any *ilāh* [god] with Allah? Little is it that you remember!﴾

(Qur'an 27: 62)

"Women should stay home, for they are fragile vessels that may easily break."

"Beware of harming others, for this is a sign of defeat."

10
❖... And whoever withholds only withholds [benefit] from himself.❖

(Qur'an 47: 38)

A well known report about Umm al-Banīn bint 'Abd al-'Azīz — the sister of 'Umar ibn 'Abd al-'Azīz — and her generosity tells how she would invite women to her house and give them fine clothes and *dinars* (Arabic money). She would say: "The clothes are for you, but the *dinars* are to be shared among your poor ones." Thus, she wanted to teach them to spend and get used to being generous. It is narrated that she used to say: "Fie on stinginess! By Allah, if it were a garment I would never wear it and if it were a road I would never follow it."

Among her sayings concerning generosity is the following:

"Everyone has been created with a strong inclination towards something, and my inclination is towards generosity. By Allah, giving to others and helping them is dearer to me than eating good food when I am hungry or having a cold drink when I am thirsty."

Because she was so keen to spend in the proper manner, and she was able to do favours to others — may Allah have mercy on her — she said:

"I have never envied anyone for anything except the one who does favours to others, for I would like to have a share in that."

Such was Umm al-Banīn, and such were her words and actions. Where are the Muslim women from her nowadays?

"In the death of selfishness lies true happiness."

Chapter 14

*... Only those who are patient shall receive
their reward in full, without reckoning.*

(Qur'an 39: 10)

1
You are a Muslim woman, neither eastern nor western

Listen to this exhortation from a German Muslim woman:

Do not be deceived by the West and its ideas and fashions. All of that is a trick to try to tempt us away from our religion gradually in order to take our wealth.

Islam and its family system is what suits women, because women, by their nature, like to stay at home. Perhaps you are asking why?

Because Allah, the Exalted, created men stronger than women, with more endurance, reason and physical strength. And He created women more emotional, with strong feelings; women do not possess the same physical strength as men. To some extent, women are moody in comparison to men. Hence, their home is the place of tranquility for them. The woman who loves her husband and children will not leave her house for no reason or mix with men at all. Ninety-nine per cent of females in the West did not reach the state of decline until they had sold themselves and had no fear of God in their hearts.

Women's going out to work in the west at this large scale caused men to play the role of women, so, they stay at home washing dishes, looking after children and drinking alcohol. I know that Islam does not object to a man helping his wife at home, indeed this is encouraged, but not to such an extent that their roles are swapped.

> "Be beautiful and you will see the world beautiful."

◆And We will ease you toward easy;...◆   *(Qur'an 87: 8)*

2
Forget your worries and keep yourself busy

If you have done what you can to deal with a problem, then distract yourself with a hobby, reading or some work. Keeping yourself busy in this situation, will take the place of anxiety, for ◆Allah has not made for any man two hearts inside his body...◆ *(cf. Qur'an 33: 4)*. Let us assume that the problem is a child's sickness. The parent (father or mother) does what he or she can to give the right medicine properly, then he or she spends the rest of his or her time doing something useful.

When faced with a current problem, it is fitting to remember difficult problems that you have gone through in the past, especially major problems that were more serious than the problem being faced now. Remember how Allah helped you to solve it, to such an extent that remembering it now brings nothing more than a smile and a feeling of self-confidence. If you can remember that, you will feel that today's problem is just like the old problem; it, too, will pass and be solved — by Allah's leave.

Seek a positive answer to your problem, and it is certainly not going to be more negative than positive. Ibn al-Jawzi spoke wise words when he said:

"Whoever is stricken by a calamity, let him imagine it as being worse than it is, and imagine its reward. Let him also imagine a calamity greater than the one befalling him.

Thus, he will realize that it is a great blessing that the calamity is no greater than what it is, and hope that it will be relieved soon. If it were not for intense calamities, no one would hope for the time of relief."

"A wise man said: 'I have never regretted what I did not say, but I have often regretted what I did say.'"

◆Our Lord! Let not our hearts deviate
[from the truth] after You have guided us...◆

(Qur'an 3: 8)

3
Points to help you find happiness

Avarice and greed are fatal, and their remedy lies in the following:

1. Economy in spending, for the one who spends a great deal will never be content, rather he will be overwhelmed by avarice and greed. Economy in spending is the basis of contentment. As the saying goes: Good management will save you half of your wealth.

2. Do not worry too much about the future, and try to focus your wishes on the short term, having faith that whatever has been decreed for you will reach you.

3. Fearing Allah, the Almighty, for Allah says:

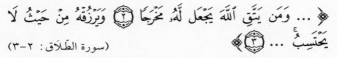

(سورة الطَّلاَق : ٢ -٣)

◆... And whosoever fears Allah [and keeps his duty to Him], He will make a way out for him [from every difficulty]. And He will provide him from [sources] he never could imagine ...◆   *(Qur'an 65: 2-3)*

4. Realizing what contentment brings of pride in being independent of means, and what greed and avarice bring of humiliation — and learning lessons from both.

5.   Contemplating the lives of the Prophets (may Allah's peace
     be upon them) and the righteous Companions of the Prophet
     Muhammad (may Allah be pleased with them all), how they
     were content and humble and how keen they were to do
     righteous deeds. Take them as your example.

6.   Look at those who are worse than you in worldly terms.

> "The wise man seeks to benefit from
> wise opinions; he never despairs or
> gives up thinking and trying."

❨Truly, Allah defends those who believe...❩

(Qur'an 22: 38)

4
Strengthen your relationship with Allah when all others fail

Righteous deeds accompanied by faith will be rewarded with a good life on earth. It does not matter whether this life is filled with luxuries and riches, for a good life may be attained with or without such things.

There are many things in life, besides great wealth, which make life good, even if one has only what is enough. For example:

A good relationship with Allah, having trust in Him, being assured of His care and good pleasure; good health, tranquility, contentment, blessings, feeling content at home and enjoying friendly relationships with others; the joy of doing righteous deeds and their effect on one's conscience and life.

Wealth is just one element, and a little of it is enough so that the heart may focus on things that are greater, purer and more lasting in the sight of Allah.

"An established rule states that great men inherit their greatness from their mothers."

❮There is no god but Allah.❯ *(Qur'an 37: 35)*

5
No one is happier than those who believe in Allah

I have read the biographies of dozens of rich and great men worldwide, who did not have faith in Allah, and I discovered that their lives ended in misery and disgrace. Where are they now? Where is the wealth and treasure that they accumulated? Where are the palaces and mansions that they built? It has all come to an end. Some of them committed suicide, others were killed, some were imprisoned and the rest were arrested and taken to court for their sins, crimes, foul play and mischief. They became the most miserable of people, when they imagined that their wealth could buy them everything — happiness, love, health and youth — then they found out that real happiness, real love, perfect health and real youth cannot be bought with money. Yes, they could buy imaginary happiness, false love and health in the marketplace, but all the wealth in the world cannot buy a heart, generate love or create joy.

No one is happier than those who believe in Allah, because they have light from their Lord, they check themselves, they do that which Allah commands and avoid that which Allah forbids. Listen to the way they are described in the Holy Qur'an:

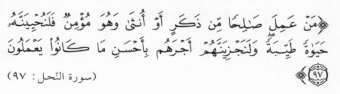

﴿مَنْ عَمِلَ صَـٰلِحًا مِّن ذَكَرٍ أَوْ أُنثَىٰ وَهُوَ مُؤْمِنٌ فَلَنُحْيِيَنَّهُۥ حَيَوٰةً طَيِّبَةً وَلَنَجْزِيَنَّهُمْ أَجْرَهُم بِأَحْسَنِ مَا كَانُوا۟ يَعْمَلُونَ﴾

(سورة النّحل: ٩٧)

❨Whoever does righteousness — whether male or
female — while he [or she] is a true believer [of
Islamic Monotheism] verily, to him We will give a
good life [in this world with respect, contentment and
lawful provision], and We shall pay them certainly a
reward in proportion to the best of what they used to
do [i.e. Paradise in the Hereafter].❩ *(Qur'an 16: 97)*

"He is not happy who does not want
to be happy."

"Everything happens by the will and decree of Allah."

6
A life with no extravagance and luxuries

The righteous Muslim woman prepares food according to need, so that nothing is left over to speak of her extravagance and bad management. Her example in this regard is the Mother of the Believers 'Ā'ishah (may Allah be pleased with her). It was narrated that 'Ā'ishah said: *"No barley bread would be left over from the meal of the Messenger of Allah, neither a little nor a lot."*

According to another report: *"When the meal was cleared away from before the Messenger of Allah, there would be no food left over."*

One of the things forbidden in Islam and regarded as extravagance, is the use of vessels of gold and silver for eating and drinking. It is narrated from Umm Salamah (may Allah be pleased with her) that the Messenger of Allah (Blessings and Peace be upon him) said: *"The one who drinks from a vessel of silver is swallowing Hellfire into his stomach."*

According to a report narrated by Imam Muslim: *"The one who eats or drinks from a vessel of gold or silver is swallowing Hellfire into his stomach."*

Indeed, Islam is wise in this prohibition, for these are luxuries that characterize those who live a life of opulence. Islam always wants its followers to be humble and to live away from luxury. The Messenger of Allah (Blessings and Peace be upon him) said to Mu'ādh ibn Jabal, when he sent him to Yemen: "Beware of luxury, for the slaves of Allah are not those who live a life of luxury."

"When you stop looking at your
internal misery, you will be happy."

"Be above reproach."

7
Doing righteous deeds rejoices the heart

'Ā'ishah (may Allah be pleased with her) said:

"A poor woman came to me with her two daughters, and I gave each of them a date. She put a date to her mouth to eat it, and her daughters asked her for more, so she split the date that she was going to eat and gave them half each. I was impressed by what she did, and I told the Messenger of Allah about it. He said: *'Allah has granted her Paradise because of this, or freed her from the Fire.'*"

Umm Salamah asked the Messenger of Allah (Blessings and Peace be upon him) about her spending on her sons. She said: "Will I have a reward with regard to the sons of Abu Salamah, if I spend on them, when I am not going to neglect them anyway because they are my children?"

She affirmed that she would not neglect them, before the Prophet (Blessings and Peace be upon him) answered in the positive. Her natural inclination answered her before he did.

Islam encourages righteous deeds, kindness towards relatives and upholding the ties of kinship. It instills compassion and love in society so that the children may grow up righteous.

"Be happy — ...here is true happiness."

*"A woman is a fragrant flower and a
sweetly-singing nightingale."*

8
Allah saves us from every difficulty

The plane was travelling at a great height, suspended between heaven and earth, when the instruments showed that something was wrong. The pilot and passengers panicked; the men wept, the women screamed and the children were terrified. Panic prevailed, and they started beseeching Allah and crying out, "O' Allah, O' Allah..." Then His mercy and compassion descended, the people calmed down and the plane landed safely.

The baby was lying in a transverse position and the delivery was difficult; the mother was sure that she was about to die. She turned to Allah, the Reliever of distress, the One Who meets all needs, and cried, "O' Allah, O' Allah..." Then her troubles ceased and her child emerged safely into the world.

The scholar was faced with a difficult issue and was confused, looking for the right answer but could not find it. He humbled himself and called out:

"O' Allah, O' Allah, O' You Who taught Ibrāhīm and caused Sulaymān to understand, help me to understand. O' Allah, Lord of Jibrīl and Mika'īl and Isrāfīl, Creator of the heavens and the earth, Knower of the unseen and the seen, You judge between Your slaves with regard to that wherein they differ, guide me to the truth concerning that wherein they differ by Your leave, for You guide whomsoever You will to the straight path." Then came divine help and the obstacles were removed. Glory be to Him, how

Merciful He is.

> "The happiest man is the one who
> makes the largest number of people
> happy."

"Fear Allah with regard to women."

(Hadith)

9

Beware of negligence

Beware of negligence, beware of forgetting to remember Allah, the Almighty, of neglecting to pray, or turning away from the Qur'an, of missing useful lectures and lessons. These are the causes of negligence, which leads to hard-heartedness and the sealing of one's heart: If that happens to a person, he will never recognize anything good or denounce anything bad and he will never understand anything about the religion of Allah; he will remain hard-hearted, confused and miserable. These are the consequences of negligence in this world, so how about the Hereafter?

So, you must avoid the causes of negligence mentioned above. Fear Allah, keep your tongue moist with the remembrance of Allah, reciting *tasbīḥ*, *tahlīl*, *takbīr* and *taḥmīd* [3]; pray for forgiveness, send blessings upon the Prophet (Blessings and Peace be upon him) at all times, when you are standing, sitting or lying on your side. Then you will find happiness filling your heart. This is the effect of *dhikr*, remembering Allah, the All-Merciful, All-Glorious.

---

[3] *Tasbīḥ*: saying, *"Subḥān Allāh* (Glory be to Allah)".
Tahlīl: saying, *"Lā ilāha illallāh* (there is no god but Allah)".
Takbīr: saying, *"Allāhu akbar* (Allah is Most Great)".
Taḥmīd: saying, *"Al-Ḥamdu lillāh* (Praise be to Allah)".

﴿ ... أَلَا بِذِكْرِ اللَّهِ تَطْمَئِنُّ الْقُلُوبُ ﴿٢٨﴾ ﴾

(سورة الرّعد: ٢٨)

﴿... Verily, in the remembrance of Allah do hearts find rest.﴾ *(Qur'an 13 :28)*

"Do not wait to be happy so that you smile but smile to be happy."

"Expect happiness, do not expect misery."

10
Smile at life

When you smile even though your heart is filled with worry, you reduce your suffering and open a door to the way out. Do not hesitate to smile, for inside you there is a kind of energy full of smiles. Beware of suppressing it, for that means that you are strangling yourself with pain and suffering. It will not harm you if you smile, even when you are talking to others about serious matters from the depths of your heart. How wonderful it is when our lips speak the language of smiles!

A westerner once said: "Smiling is a social obligation," and he was right, because if you want to mix with people, you have to be nice to them. You have to understand that social life requires human skills at which you have to be proficient, one of which is smiling. This is a social phenomenon which is common to all people. When you smile at people, you are sharing the beauty of life and the spirit of optimism with them; you are giving them the glad tidings of the best that they can hope for. But if you meet them with a face that is devoid of compassion, you are tormenting them and disturbing them with such appearance. How can you accept to be the cause of other people's misery?

"Glory is not granted except to those who always dreamed of it."

EPILOGUE

And Now

After reading this book, you may dismiss grief, desert anxiety, depart the locations of depression and evacuate the tents of despair and frustration to come to the *mihrab* of faith, the Ka'bah of intimity with God and to the rank of satisfaction with His decree and pre-destination in order to begin a new life but a happy one, different days but nice ones; life without hesitation, worry or confusion and days without boredom or weariness. Once this happens, the caller of faith will call you from above the mountain of hope, in the valley of contentment to hail the glad tidings: *"You are (The Happiest Woman in the world)"*.

AUTHOR'S BIOGRAPHY

'Ā'iḍ ibn 'Abd-Allah ibn 'Ā'iḍ Āl Majdū' al-Qarni

► Born 1379 AH

► Obtained his Batchelor's degree from the College of Uṣūl ad-Dīn in Imam Muhammad ibn Sa'ūd Islamic University.

► Obtained his Master's degree in Prophetic Hadith in 1408 AH. The title of his thesis was *al-Bid'ah wa Atharuha fid-Dirāyah war-Riwāyah* (Innovation and its effects on Understanding and Reporting).

► Obtained his Doctorate from Imām Muhammad ibn Sa'ūd Islamic University in 1422 AH, with a thesis entitled *al-Mufahhim lima ashkala min Talkhīṣ Ṣaḥīḥ Muslim li al-Qurṭubi — Dirāsah wa Taḥqīq* (Explanation of difficult passages in al-Qurṭubi's *Summary of Ṣaḥīḥ Muslim — A study*).

► He has recorded more than 800 audiocassettes of *khuṭbahs* (sermons), lessons, lectures and soirees.

► He has written on hadith, *tafsīr*, *fiqh*, Arabic literature, *sīrah* and biography.

► He has attended dozens of lectures and soirees, and has attended conferences organized by the Muslim Arab Youth Association (MAYA) and the Qur'an and Sunnah society in the USA. He also lectured at literary and sports clubs, universities and seminars.

GLOSSARY

Al-Qaḍā' wal-Qadar	القضاء والقدر :	Fate and Divine Decree
A'ūdhu	اعوذُ :	I seek refuge
'Awrah	عورة :	for men: from the navel to the knees, and for women: entire body except the face and hands
Bid'ah	بدعة :	Heresy, reprehensible innovation in religion
Dā'iyah	داعية :	Caller to Islam
Da'wah	دعوة :	Call to Islam
Dhikr	ذِكر :	Remembrance of Allah the Exalted, *Dhikr* is the also used for the Qur'an
Hadith	حديث :	Record of Prophetic sayings and actions
Ḥalāl	حلال :	Legal, lawful, Islamically permissible
Ḥarām	حرام :	Illegal, unlawful, prohibited
Ḥijāb	حِجاب :	Islamic (legal) dress for women, veil, cover
Imam	إمام :	Leader in prayers, scholar in religion

'Ishā'	عِشاء :	Early night (evening) prayer
Jāhiliyah	جاهلية :	Pre-Islamic era, ignorance, non-Islamic
Jihād	جِهاد :	Struggle, striving for Islamic order, fighting in the cause of Allah
Kāfir	كافِر :	Disbeliever, unbeliever
Khuṭbah	خُطبه :	Religious sermon, speech
Kufr	كُفر :	Disbelief
Maḥram	محرم :	A person unmarriageable due to close blood-relationship
Nawāfil	نوافِل :	Sing. *Nafl*; Voluntary prayer, fasting, alms, etc.
Ramaḍān	رمضان :	The month of Fasting, the ninth Hijri month
Salaf	سلف :	Predecessors, early righteous generation
Sīrah	سيرة :	Biography — particularly of Prophet Muhammad (bpuh)
Ṭabaqāt	طبقات :	Classes (of society), layers, also name of a book on *Ṣaḥābah*
Tahajjud	تهجُّد :	Supereragatory worship (prayer) at night till *fajr* prayer
Tahlīl	تهليل :	Saying, "*Lā ilāha illallah*": There is no god except Allah
Taḥmīd	تحميد :	Saying, "*al-Ḥamdu lillah*": Praise is due to Allah

Takbīr	تكبير :	Saying "*Allahu akbar*": Allah is the Greatest
Ṭalāq	طلاق :	Divorce
Taqwa	تقوى :	Piety, righteousness
Tasbīḥ	تسبيح :	Saying "*Subhan Allah*": Glorified is Allah
Ṭayyibāt	طيبات :	Lawful food and drink, also: delicacies
Wuḍū'	وضوء :	Ablution
Zakāh	زكوه / زكاة :	Obligatory annual fixed charity — Poor-due on every Muslim possessing wealth over a certain limit, a pillar of Islam

TRANSLITERATION CHART

أ	a
آ . ى	ā
ب	b
ت	t
ة	h or t (when followed by another Arabic word)
ث	th
ج	j
ح	ḥ
خ	kh
د	d
ذ	dh
ر	r
ز	z
س	s
ش	sh
ص	ṣ
ض	ḍ
ط	ṭ

ظ	ẓ
ع	'
غ	gh
ف	f
ق	q
ك	k
ل	l
م	m
ن	n
هـ – ه – ـه	h
و	w
و (as vowel)	ū
ي	y
ي (as vowel)	ī
ء	' (Omitted in initial position)

´	Fatḥah	a
ِ	Kasra	i
ُ	Ḍammah	u
ّ	Shaddah	Double letter
°	Sukūn	Absence of vowel

LIST OF CONTENTS

PUBLISHER'S NOTE   5

DEDICATION   7

TRANSLATOR'S FOREWORD   9

INTRODUCTION   11

CHAPTER 1   15

  WELCOME!   17

  YES!   18

  NO!   19

  TEN THOUGHTS TO PONDER   20

  THINK ABOUT IT...   22

CHAPTER 2   23

  1 - A woman who challenged tyranny   25

  2 - You have a huge wealth of blessings   27

  3 - It is sufficient honour for you that you are a Muslim   29

  4 - The believing woman and the disbelieving
      woman are not equal   31

  5 - Laziness is kin to failure   33

  6 - You are better off than millions of women   34

  7 - Build yourself a palace in Paradise   36

  8 - Do not destroy your heart with your own hands   37

9 - You are dealing with a Lord Who is
    Most Kind and Most Generous   39

10 - You will be the winner in all situations   42

CHAPTER 3   43

1 - Count the blessings that Allah
    has bestowed upon you   45

2 - A little that makes you happy is better than
    a lot that makes you miserable   46

3 - Look at the clouds and not at the ground   47

4 - Living in a hut with faith is better than
    living in a palace with disbelief   48

5 - Organize your time so that you can
    do all you have to do   49

6 - Our happiness is not like theirs   50

7 - Climb aboard the ship of salvation   51

8 - The key to happiness is prostration   52

9 - Old women make heroes   53

10 - To be the most beautiful woman in the world   54

CHAPTER 4   55

1 - You are notable and honourable   57

2 - Accept the blessing and make the most of it   58

3 - A great deal of provision comes with
    seeking forgiveness   60

4 - Du'ā' (invocation) relieves distress   61

5 - Beware of despair and frustration   63

6 - Your house is a kingdom of glory and love   64

7 - You do not have time for idle talk   65

8 - Be cheerful at heart and the universe
   will embrace you   66
9 - No one is ever completely happy   68
10 - Enter the garden of knowledge   70

CHAPTER 5   71

1 - Remember the shed tears and broken hearts   73
2 - These people are not happy   74
3 - The way to Allah is the best way   75
4 - When things become unbearable, turn to Allah 77
5 - Make every day a new beginning   79
6 - Women are like stars in the sky   81
7 - Death is preferable to doing *ḥarām*
   (forbidden) actions   83
8 - Inspiring verses   85
9 - Knowledge of the Most Merciful takes away grief 87
10 - The blessed day   89

CHAPTER 6   91

1 - A wise woman is the source of a happy life   93
2 - Take care of today only   94
3 - Do not feel that everyone is out to get you 96
4 - How sweet is success after hardship   98
5 - You will adapt to your situation and cope with it 99
6 - Sound advice from a wise woman   101
7 - A woman who offered herself as a sacrifice
   and thus earned the pleasure of her Lord   103

8 - She adhered to the commands of Allah and
    Allah protected her   105

9 - The water of repentance is the purest water   107

10 - The first freedom fighter   109

CHAPTER 7   111

1 - Put your trust in your Lord   113

2 - Blindness of the heart is real blindness   115

3 - Do not try to establish a court of vengeance,
    for you may be the first victim   117

4 - Distinction is earned by achievement   119

5 - The world of *kufr* is suffering from misery   120

6 - The attitude of a life-partner   121

7 - Be content with what Allah has decreed for you   122

8 - Do not feel any regret about this world   124

9 - The most wondrous beauty lies in
    the creation of Allah   125

10 - The ultimate honour and infinite generosity   127

CHAPTER 8   129

1 - You have nowhere to turn but to Allah   131

2 - Happiness exists... but who can find it?   133

3 - A good attitude is a great blessing   134

4 - How to achieve a happy life   136

5 - Seek refuge with Allah from worry and grief   138

6 - The woman who offers support at
    the time of calamity   140

7 - A woman from among the people of Paradise   141

8 - Charity wards off calamity   142

9 - Be beautiful in spirit because the
    universe is beautiful   143

10 - A hero Woman   144

CHAPTER 9   145

1 - Do not spend your time doing nothing   147

2 - Happiness cannot be bought with money   148

3 - Haste and recklessness are the fuel of misery   150

4 - The game of accumulating wealth has no end   151

5 - Immorality is generated by idleness   152

6 - A house without anger, noise and exhaustion   154

7 - Chastity and modesty enhance beauty   155

8 - Allah may bring the absent person back home   157

9 - One phrase may fill time and space   159

10 - Hearts longing for Paradise   160

CHAPTER 10   161

1 - Belief in the divine will and decree,
    both good and bad   163

2 - The best things are those that are moderate   165

3 - The pessimist creates an atmosphere of depression   166

4 - Beware of complaining and being discontent   167

5 - Most problems have petty causes   168

6 - Restraining the tongue   169

7 - Fight anxiety by praying   171

8 - Advice of a successful woman   173

9 - Whoever does not find comfort in Allah
    will not find comfort in anything else   175

10 - She of the Two Girdles lived two lives   177

CHAPTER 11   179

1 - Who is the dearest beloved?   181

2 - Happiness has nothing to do with
    richness or poverty   182

3 - Is not Allah more deserving of thanks
    than anyone else?   183

4 - The happy woman makes those
    around her happy, too   184

5 - Be content, for everything happens by
    the will and decree of Allah   185

6 - Umm 'Amārah speaks   187

7 - Kindness to others washes away grief   188

8 - Turn your losses into gains   190

9 - Sincerity is very precious; where are
    the sincere ones?   191

10 - Be serious, be serious...   193

CHAPTER 12   195

1 - Take a brave stance when you check yourself   197

2 - Beware!   199

3 - Being grateful to the beneficent is a duty   200

4 - The soul deserves more care than the body   202

5 - Keep busy with the present rather
    than the past or future   203

6 - Calamities are means of attaining desires   205

7 - Show mercy to those who are on earth and the
        One Who is in heaven will show mercy to you   207

8 - The beautiful world is seen only by optimists   209

9 - Acknowledge Allah at times of ease and
        He will help you at times of hardship   210

10 - The woman with the highest dowry in the world 212

CHAPTER 13   215

1 - The keys to victory   217

2 - After suffering comes the joy of victory   218

3 - Anxiety exhausts the body and the mind   220

4 - Your loved job is the secret of your happiness   222

5 - Strength is in the spirit, not in the body   223

6 - A great woman turns a hell of calamity
        into a paradise   225

7 - Be patient to be victorious   226

8 - In hardships, we have no refuge
        except Allah Alone   227

9 - Is not He (better than your gods) Who responds
        to the distressed one, when he calls on Him? 229

10 - ﴾... And whoever withholds only withholds
        [benefit] from himself.﴿   231

CHAPTER 14   233

1 - You are a Muslim woman, neither
        eastern nor western   235

2 - Forget your worries and keep yourself busy   237

3 - Points to help you find happiness   239

4 - Strengthen your relationship with Allah
     when all others fail   241

5 - No one is happier than those who believe in Allah 242

6 - A life with no extravagance and luxuries   244

7 - Doing righteous deeds rejoices the heart   246

8 - Allah saves us from every difficulty   247

9 - Beware of negligence   249

10 - Smile at life   251

EPILOGUE   253

AUTHOR'S BIOGRAPHY   255

GLOSSARY   257

TRANSLITERATION CHART   261

LIST OF CONTENTS   263

NOTES

NOTES